The Macat Library

世界思想宝库钥匙丛书

解析瓦尔特·本雅明

《机械复制时代的艺术作品》

AN ANALYSIS OF

WALTER BENJAMIN'S

THE WORK OF ART IN THE AGE OF MECHANICAL REPRODUCTION

Rachele Dini ◎ 著

顾忆青 ◎ 译

上海外语教育出版社
外教社 SHANGHAI FOREIGN LANGUAGE EDUCATION PRESS

MACAT

目　录

CONTENTS

引言

要 点

- 瓦尔特·本雅明是德国犹太裔左翼哲学家，代表作有《机械复制时代的艺术作品》[1]和《历史哲学论纲》[2]。
- 《机械复制时代的艺术作品》旨在考察艺术、推动艺术创作的技术革新，及其与政治三者之间的关系。
- 该文为第二次世界大战 * 之后学界有关新兴媒介、文化和政治的探讨奠定了基础。

瓦尔特·本雅明其人

瓦尔特·本雅明是德国犹太裔哲学家，其著作主要探讨资本主义对艺术、政治和社会生活所产生的影响，至今仍具有极为重要的学术价值。1892 年，本雅明出生于柏林，他从小家境富裕，但成年以后却饱经困苦。本雅明的早期思想深受教育改革家古斯塔夫·维内肯 * 的影响。当时他正在维内肯创办的寄宿学校读书。维内肯是激进 * 青年杂志《开端》的编辑，这份杂志是知识青年运动的宣传阵地，主要传播黑格尔、歌德、康德和尼采等 18、19 世纪德国哲学家的理想。

本雅明先后在弗莱堡大学、柏林大学和慕尼黑大学修读哲学，并于 1919 年获得伯尔尼大学博士学位。在慕尼黑求学期间，他与哲学家哥舒姆·舒勒姆 * 相识，并成为一生的挚友。在舒勒姆的引荐下，他开始研究犹太神秘主义 * 思想。然而，本雅明真正走上哲学道路是在 1923 年——社会研究所 * 成立之时。正是在那里，他遇见了西奥多·阿多诺 *、格奥尔格·卢卡奇 * 等哲学家。他们的论著（尤其是卢卡奇 1920 年所作的《小说理论》）对本雅明的创作产生了深刻影响。

《机械复制时代的艺术作品》首稿完成于 1935 年末。当时，本雅明被纳粹政权驱逐出境，且被剥夺德国国籍，不得已而移居巴黎。该文的法语修订译本随后由社会研究所出版。这个以马克思主义研究为核心的学术团体，为躲避纳粹迫害，已从法兰克福大学迁往纽约。文中有关卡尔·马克思*的引文皆被编辑删除，以免众多拥护资本主义的美国民众产生敌意。该文现今最为通行的版本是本雅明 1939 年的重写本，时值欧洲深陷第二次世界大战之际。大约一年后，本雅明在逃避盖世太保*的追捕时自杀，但死因成谜。直至 1968 年，这篇重写本的英译版才得以问世。

《机械复制时代的艺术作品》的主要内容

在《机械复制时代的艺术作品》中，瓦尔特·本雅明指出，传统艺术批评*理论所强调的"创造性与天赋、永恒价值与神秘"等诸多概念都已过时。其原因有二：一是新艺术形式的出现，如摄影术和电影，受众集体观赏而获得个人体验，其过程有别于欣赏绘画和戏剧；二是法西斯主义*在欧洲的兴起，通过操纵戏剧化和艺术化的修辞话语来影响公共舆论。

本雅明认为，面对法西斯领袖蛊惑人心的视觉冲击，熟悉电影艺术的观众被煽动的可能性很低，既难以动摇其观点，亦无法使其忽视社会不公。电影成为一种抗争手段，能够反抗本雅明所称的"政治美学化*"，因为电影能使大众分神获得消遣，故而亦可反之用于摆脱宣传攻势的干扰。本雅明提出一系列全新概念，旨在理解新技术时代艺术的接受面貌，藉此挖掘艺术的革命潜力。他所强调的这些概念"迥异于其他更广为人知的（艺术理论）术语，因为它们对于推行法西斯主义毫无作用。但从另一方面而言，这些概念对于形塑艺术政治领域的变革需求却大有裨益。"

本雅明指出，在法西斯主义者眼中，观众对于一件艺术作品有其固定的接受模式，无论何时何地观赏皆是如此；所以，艺术作品的价值和内涵永恒不变。共产主义者则认为，推动艺术作品生产的社会、文化和政治语境交织着诸种作用力。他们坚信，一件艺术作品的内涵及其接受模式随时间而变化；因而，即便是艺术作品自身的历史，都在不断被重释。在本雅明看来，机械复制时代的艺术作品深刻揭示了现实如何以全新的方式重塑过去：例如，电影以崭新的面貌重构莎士比亚戏剧的内涵，赋予既定的文本表达以新的生命。倘若过去并非一成不变，那么现实亦是如此。这意味着变革具有可能性：本雅明指出，我们可以改变技术的构成方式，不仅用以艺术生产，还能反抗压迫统治。

本雅明的这篇论著在其有生之年并未产生多少影响，且出版十年间亦未引起广泛关注。然而，自 20 世纪 60 年代末以来，这篇论著在艺术批评、文化研究和文学理论等领域产生了巨大轰动。《机械复制时代的艺术作品》中的诸多观点，成为众多有关 20 世纪文学和艺术批评理论著作的灵感源泉，包括约翰·伯格 * 广受推崇的艺术批评论著《观看之道》（1977）和苏珊·桑塔格 * 的文论作品《论摄影》（1977）等。近年来，不少新闻传播学者也引用本雅明的这篇论著，以及他的哲学家挚友西奥多·阿多诺和麦克斯·霍克海默 * 的著作，来分析 2016 年美国总统大选。有评论家认为，此次选举的结果归因于唐纳德·特朗普 * 对社交媒体的操纵，加之运用脱离现实的戏剧化修辞话语。还有一些评论家甚至宣称，本雅明及其同仁"早已预知特朗普的出现"——这虽是耸人听闻的断言，却得以解释公众为何对他们的思想重新产生兴趣。

《机械复制时代的艺术作品》的学术价值

技术革新、艺术生产、政治和公共生活四者之间的关系，是人文和社会科学领域的焦点议题。而《机械复制时代的艺术作品》正是理解相关思想论争的扛鼎之作，至今仍具启迪意义。本雅明在文中剖析了电影、摄影术及其接受模式可能对公众产生的影响；他还提出，载体与内容同等重要，由此推动媒介理论的发展。本雅明所关注的问题是，一件艺术作品的可复制性如何影响我们对其价值的判断？它以何种方式使人人享有观赏的机会，并将观众转变为参与者？这些思考极大地促进了当前有关互联网和用户生成内容＊的探讨，揭示了其潜在的民主化特征。同时，他还希望，新兴媒介的出现能使艺术批评走向新形式，从而向现状发起挑战。如今人们对于博客、脸书和推特的激进意义争论不休，正与之形成共鸣。

《机械复制时代的艺术作品》亦为全面了解本雅明的思想指明方向。本雅明一生著述颇丰，论题深邃而广泛，涵盖历史、政治、艺术、文学和宗教等众多领域，其中最广为人知的，便是他对资本主义的剖析，探究其对文化和社会的影响。他离经叛道的论述，游走在不同学科之间，读来常常令人捉摸不透，难以归类——然而，这也正是为何本雅明的思想对不同领域的学者都具有参考价值的缘由所在。事实上，相较于哲学，他的思想在文学和文化批评界更具影响力，充分体现其开放性和普适性：从某种程度上而言，本雅明所谈论的那个社会，与我们身处的全球化数字时代仍密不可分。他有关艺术、科技和权力的诸多观点，依然与21世纪的世界息息相关。《机械复制时代的艺术作品》在学界意义深远。不仅如此，但凡论及当今政治话语的对立和分裂，探讨新兴媒介和艺术对公共生活的影响，这篇论著皆可谓是经典范本。

---

1. 瓦尔特·本雅明："机械复制时代的艺术作品"，《启迪》，汉娜·阿伦特编，伦敦：皮姆里科出版社，1999年。

2. 瓦尔特·本雅明："历史哲学论纲"，《启迪》，汉娜·阿伦特编，伦敦：皮姆里科出版社，1999年。

第一部分：学术渊源

1 作者生平与历史背景

要点 ⚷

- 《机械复制时代的艺术作品》是艺术批评、文学研究 * 和批判理论 * 史上的扛鼎之作。

- 瓦尔特·本雅明是犹太裔左翼知识分子，逝世数十年后其重要价值才广受认可。

- 本雅明的这篇论著成稿于二战前夕最动荡的岁月。

为何要读这部著作？

哲学家、文化批评家本雅明在其影响深远的论著《机械复制时代的艺术作品》中提出一系列全新的观点来理解现代艺术作品。本雅明重新审视艺术史 * 和艺术批评的传统观点，指出艺术作品必须置于其诞生之际（艺术作品如何制成）的物质史中加以理解，且需考虑观众的全新接受模式。本雅明强调，摄影术和电影等新兴媒介意义非凡，使艺术作品具有可复制性和可传播性，而观众通常也以群体形式体验其中，这与欣赏绘画或观摩戏剧截然不同。

本雅明认为，可复制性致使艺术作品的"灵晕" * 消逝：机械复制时代的艺术作品并非处于孤立自律的空间（当时的艺术史学者如是认为），而是遍布生活的角角落落。这一论述极为重要，因为在本雅明看来，坚称艺术具有自律性 * 的观点，与法西斯主义者的宣传辞藻别无二致，都是将一己之见强加于人，将社会不公视为"自然而然"，并将生活本身看作一件永恒不变的艺术作品。与之相反，认为艺术是政治时局的产物且具有变化性的观点，则能使我们窥见艺术的革命潜力。尽管本雅明的这篇论著在出版后的三十年里并未引起重视，但自 20 世纪 70 年代以来，却对文学艺术批评和文化研究 * 产生了巨大影响。2016 年起，这篇论著还被新闻记者广为引用，用以分析美国总统大选和极端右翼势力的兴起。[1]

> "（本雅明）在亲笔书写中获得的愉悦之感……堪比他对机器打字的厌恶之情：由此可见，《机械复制时代的艺术作品》正如他其他创作阶段的论作一样，旨在辨别这种巨大差异。"
>
> —— 西奥多 · 阿多诺：《书信作家本雅明》

作者生平

瓦尔特 · 本雅明（1892—1940）是德国犹太裔左翼哲学家，出生于柏林一个富庶家庭。他父亲既是银行家，又是一位艺术品商人。在他父亲看来，本雅明根本不用另谋生计，因为其财富足够支持儿子度过余生。正如汉娜 · 阿伦特 * 所言，这种与生俱来的社会地位和经济特权，是 19 世纪末德国犹太裔知识分子的共同特征。在父母资助下，他们能够安心求学写作。[2] 然而，与富裕的少年时代形成鲜明反差的是，本雅明成年以后却饱经困苦。第一次世界大战 * 使德国陷入经济萧条（史称"大萧条" * 时期），他的父亲再也无力承担他和妻子朵拉 · 苏菲 · 波拉客 * 的生活开支。于是，此后的数十年间，本雅明挣扎着靠写作为生。[3] 经济上的窘迫也使其婚姻深受影响。这段婚姻仅持续了 11 年：1918 年，他和朵拉的儿子降生；而在 1928 年，两人便宣告离婚。

一战期间，本雅明沉浸在诗人夏尔 · 波德莱尔 * 作品的翻译之中。波德莱尔由此成为他的思想源泉，使他对资本主义*、城市化*和艺术之间的关系产生了浓厚兴趣——这反映在他的多篇论作中，如《巴黎，19世纪的首都》（1935；1939）和《论波德莱尔的几个主题》。后者原本还被列入他的鸿篇巨制《拱廊街计划》（1927—）*。这一计划旨在研究巴黎商业拱廊街*，但终成未竟之作。本雅明翻译的波德莱尔作品出版成书，题为《夏尔·波德莱尔：巴黎风光》（1923）*。

创作背景

《机械复制时代的艺术作品》是创作于法西斯当政时期的一部反法西斯论著。1933年2月，德国国会大厦*整幢楼毁于火焚。新近当选的德国总理阿道夫·希特勒*是一位反犹*反共分子和激进的民族主义政客。他利用国会纵火案一事，通过紧急法令来围剿其共产党政敌（这起火灾疑似由一名共产党叛乱者所为），并最终巩固其国家社会主义德国工人党*——即纳粹党的统治，使之占据国会绝对多数席位。本雅明亲眼目睹这场政治变革引发的暴力冲突愈演愈烈，于是在1933年3月流亡海外。整个20世纪30年代，他几乎都在巴黎度过，当时尚且还有足够资金。期间，他在欧洲各国广泛游历，经常与老友故交相见，为其写作寻求资助。《机械复制时代的艺术作品》的两个版本皆是在他旅居巴黎时完成——第一稿写于1935年，最终稿则于1939年完成，在此之前，他刚被纳粹政权剥夺德国国籍。[4]

1940年纳粹攻占法国，不久之后，本雅明的大批私人藏书和许多未完成的手稿都被盖世太保查抄，使他不得不逃离法国。他将当时正在写作《拱廊街计划》的相关笔记托付给作家乔治·巴代伊*，后者当时是法国国家图书馆的馆员。本雅明原本打算穿过法国和西班牙的边境小镇波尔特沃，使用西班牙过境签证从西班牙前往里斯本，再从那里乘船逃往纽约。他当时在马赛以德国难民的身份，得到美国政府签发的紧急签证。然而，一系列的不幸事件导致他的计划最终失败。据说，1940 年 9 月 26 日夜晚，当本雅明得知西班牙警察不承认他在马赛获得的签证以后，便自杀身亡。颇为讽刺的是，他的自杀之举使边境警察大为震动，于是同意其同行者进入西班牙，几周之后签证禁令宣布解除。[5] 来自法西斯主义的威胁，笼罩着那个年代，最终夺去了本雅明的生命——这一切都成为《机械复制时代的艺术作品》这篇论著重要的历史注脚。

1. 汤姆·惠曼："解读 2016 年的最佳哲学是什么？"，《异视异色》，2016 年 12 月 15 日，登录日期 2017 年 6 月 20 日，https://www.vice.com/en_uk/article/z4ngy4/which-philosophy-can-help-us-understand-2016；杰里米·罗斯："特朗普胜选说明自由秩序正摇摇欲坠"，《咆哮》，2016 年 11 月 9 日，登录日期 2017 年 6 月 20 日，https://roarmag.org/essays/trump-victory-legitimation-crisis-capitalism/；斯图尔特·杰弗里斯："20 世纪 30 年代对资本主义的批判已被遗忘，为何又重新流行起来"，《卫报》，2016 年 9 月 9 日，登录日期 2017 年 6 月 20 日，https://www.theguardian.com/books/2016/sep/09/marxist-critique-capitalism-frankfurt-school-cultural-apocalypse；亚历克斯·罗斯："法兰克福学派预知特朗普的出现"，《纽约客》，2016 年 12 月 5 日，登录日期 2017 年 6 月 20 日，http://www.newyorker.com/culture/cultural-comment/the-frankfurt-school-knew-trump-was-coming。

2. 汉娜·阿伦特："简介：瓦尔特·本雅明，1892—1940 年"（1968 年），《启迪》，哈里·佐恩译，汉娜·阿伦特编，伦敦：皮姆里科出版社，1999 年（1970 年），第 7—60 页（第 31 页）。

3. 霍华德·艾兰和迈克尔·W.詹宁斯:《瓦尔特·本雅明:批判的一生》,马萨诸塞州,坎布里奇:贝尔纳普出版社/哈佛大学出版社,2013年,第3页;第221页;第412页。

4. 罗尔夫·戈贝尔:"简介:本雅明其人",《瓦尔特·本雅明论著指南》,罗尔夫·戈贝尔编,伦敦:卡姆登书屋,2009年,第1—22页(第6页)。

5. 阿伦特:"简介:瓦尔特·本雅明,1892—1940年",第23页。

2 学术背景

要点 ⚷━━

- 《机械复制时代的艺术作品》以西方马克思主义*、超现实主义*和达达主义*为理论支撑，并对未来主义展开驳斥。

- 虽然本雅明的许多同仁都撰文反抗法西斯主义和资本主义意识形态，但并不是所有学者都像他那样对大众文化*持乐观态度。

- 本雅明的学术思想受到哲学家西奥多·阿多诺、麦克斯·霍克海默，以及戏剧家贝托尔特·布莱希特*的影响。

著作语境

《机械复制时代的艺术作品》融合诸多学科的思想观点，来探讨艺术、政治和文化等领域的关键议题，所以很难加以归类。不过，文中涉及的主要理论思潮是西方马克思主义*、达达主义、超现实主义和未来主义。

马克思主义评论家以政治哲学家卡尔·马克思的著作为依托，通过考察物质生产环境来分析与之相关的文化现象。他们共同关切的问题是，资本主义如何协调人与人、人与场所，以及人与事物之间的关系。格奥尔格·卢卡奇拓展了马克思有关商品拜物教[*1]的观点——即资本主义制度下的人际关系呈现商品交换的特征。他指出，在资本主义社会中，商品被看得比作为生产者的人更重要。[2]本雅明的这篇论著即是对卢卡奇这一观点的延伸。但与之不同的是，本雅明发现，艺术作品"灵晕"的消逝，使革命成为可能。

超现实主义和达达主义是20世纪20年代文学和视觉艺术领域

相互关联的两场运动思潮[3]。本雅明在文中对此展开了详细论述，其观点深受马克思主义思想的影响。艺术家们试图创作出惊世骇俗的作品，继而将观众从寻常生活中震醒，迫使其重新审视已知的一切。正如当时的马克思主义评论家所言，这些艺术家的所作所为旨在挑战资本主义文化。在他们眼中，资本主义文化使大众变成消费公民，如行尸走肉一般，不敢挑战政治权威，并且丧失对自身生活方式的质疑。本雅明在文中直截了当地评论达达主义者的惊人之举，视其为善用电影特殊效果的先锋派。

未来主义是一场兴起于意大利的艺术运动，几乎与超现实主义和达达主义同时出现。然而，后两者秉持社会主义*立场，前者则充斥着民族主义*和法西斯主义论调，时有暴力发生。尤为突出的是，未来主义者将速度、技术和资本主义进步视为工具，从而使意大利登上国际舞台，成为世界领袖。众所周知，他们称战争是"世界唯一的洁身之道"[4]——惟有通过暴力才能摧毁旧式传统，迎来变革。本雅明批判"政治美学化"——即举行仪式，营造"景观"，迫使大众效忠国家政权，忽视自身苦痛——同时也在质疑未来主义者对这些手段的推崇。

> "纵观各种艺术形式的历史，都曾经历过批判的时代。此时，某种艺术形式追求的效果，只有通过一种经过变革的技术标准，才能充分获得……达达主义者企图通过图像——和文字——手段，去创造公众如今在电影中寻求的效果。"
>
> ——瓦尔特·本雅明：《机械复制时代的艺术作品》

学科概览

　　本雅明的学术视角颇具新意。然而，面对法西斯主义的崛起，以及资本主义对文化的影响，他并非孤身一人直面挑战。事实上，他在麦克斯·霍克海默和西奥多·阿多诺领导下的社会研究所工作，这是个由马克思主义学者组成的反法西斯团体，本雅明是成员之一。这群在社会研究所工作的学者，如今被称为"法兰克福学派*"，因其成立地点在法兰克福大学而得名。1934 年，研究所为逃避纳粹迫害而迁往纽约。除了出版《机械复制时代的艺术作品》之外，研究所还资助本雅明完成其他几部论著。

　　法兰克福学派最广为人知的作品，也许就是阿多诺和霍克海默合著的《启蒙辩证法：哲学断片》（1947）。其中有篇题为《文化工业：作为大众欺骗的启蒙》*的文章，与本雅明的《机械复制时代的艺术作品》主题相似，但其观点是：流行文化使大众成为被动的消费者，而非具有批判意识和政治参与感的公民。流行电影和小说只是不断重复同样的主题和故事，因为这种模式化的创作能够谋取高额利润，并且屡试不爽。这一切最终导致的结果是，艺术在这样的社会背景下被视为消费品。这一论断与本雅明的看法截然不同。当时，本雅明将新兴媒介视为反抗法西斯主义的潜在手段，而阿多诺却不抱希望：他认为，摄影和电影艺术早已被征用*，用于麻痹大众意识，使之屈服膜拜。电影并不能令观众感到震颤，他们根本无法意识到自己正处于压迫之中；相反，电影能使人们脱离现实，反而正满足资本主义的需要，因为看完电影的观众心满意足地回到家中，继而再度安于现状。尽管这部论文集在本雅明逝后才出版问世，但阿多诺已在与本雅明的多次通信中表达过上述部分观点。信中，他还批评《机械复制时代的艺术作品》写得过于乐观。[5]

学术渊源

德国马克思主义戏剧家贝托尔特·布莱希特曾于20世纪20年代后期与本雅明相识，他的思想也对本雅明的创作产生了深刻影响。据汉娜·阿伦特所述，本雅明称赞布莱希特是"这个（20）世纪德国最伟大的诗人"。6 在本雅明看来，布莱希特堪称楷模，诠释了什么才是时代所需的艺术家："他洞悉时代风云，且全心投入其中。"7 他的意思是，布莱希特已经对法西斯主义抬头的严峻形势有所觉察，意识到未受约束的资本主义将带来威胁，而他将坚定地与之抗争——这正是本雅明在《机械复制时代的艺术作品》中所推崇的精神。

本雅明写过一系列有关布莱希特的评论文章，直至他逝世以后——1966年才得以发表。他在文中论述了"定格*"的重要意义：布莱希特在其戏剧作品里将情节中断，迫使观众"表达态度"8，其方式是，"让在场者出现"，"通过思考（使观众）长时间地疏离（他们所）沉浸的状态"。9 本雅明在《机械复制时代的艺术作品》中也表达过类似观点，即艺术应使我们展开批判性反思，但避免陷入自我沉醉的冥想之中。

最后，19世纪末奥地利艺术史学家阿洛伊斯·李格尔*的著作，尤其是李格尔在《罗马晚期的工艺美术》（1905）*一书中所采用的研究方法，对本雅明影响颇深。依本雅明之见，李格尔的著作之所以如此出众，是因为他认为应同时透过更为传统的审美视角——例如类型*或技巧*，来考察艺术家所身处的市场有何特征。10 由于李格尔对艺术生产环境更感兴趣，因此十分关注那些通常被艺术史学家忽视的艺术作品。而在他眼中，那些作品都是至关重要的文化产物。这一有违传统的观点，成为本雅明这篇论著中的一项关键议题。

1. 卡尔·马克思："商品的拜物教性质及其秘密"，《资本论：缩编本》，大卫·麦克莱伦编，牛津：牛津大学出版社，2008 年（1867 年），第 42—50 页。

2. 格奥尔格·卢卡奇：《历史与阶级意识：关于马克思主义辩证法的研究》，伦敦：梅林出版社，1968 年（1923 年），第 83 页。

3. 瓦尔特·本雅明："超现实主义"（1929 年），重刊于《〈单向街〉与其他作品》，阿米特·乔杜里编，J.A. 安德伍德译，伦敦：企鹅出版集团，2009 年，第 143—160 页；瓦尔特·本雅明："梦幻的媚俗：超现实主义概览"（1925 年），重刊于《〈技术可复制时代的艺术作品〉与其他作品》，迈克尔·W. 詹宁斯等编，埃德蒙·杰弗科特、罗德尼·利文斯通、霍华德·艾兰等译，马萨诸塞州坎布里奇：贝尔纳普出版社 / 哈佛大学出版社，2008 年，第 236—239 页。

4. 托马索·马里内蒂："未来主义宣言"（1908 年），《现代艺术理论：艺术家与评论家资料集》，赫谢尔·B. 奇普编，加利福尼亚州，伯克利：加利福尼亚大学出版社，1996 年（1968 年），第 286 页。

5. 西奥多·W. 阿多诺和瓦尔特·本雅明：《通信全集：1928—1940 年》，尼古拉斯·沃克译，剑桥：政体出版社，1999 年，第 127—134 页。

6. 艾德穆特·维茨斯拉：《瓦尔特·本雅明与贝托尔特·布莱希特：友谊的故事》，克里斯汀·舒特沃斯译，纽黑文：耶鲁大学出版社，第 103 页。

7. 维茨斯拉：《瓦尔特·本雅明与贝托尔特·布莱希特》，第 103 页。

8. 瓦尔特·本雅明：《理解布莱希特》，安娜·博斯托克译，伦敦：维尔索出版社，1998 年，第 100 页。

9. 本雅明：《理解布莱希特》，第 100 页。

10. T.Y. 列文："瓦尔特·本雅明与艺术史理论"，《十月》第 47 期（1988 年冬季号），第 77—83 页；迈克尔·古布斯特：《时间的可见性：阿洛伊斯·李格尔与〈世纪末的维也纳〉中的历史和时间话语》，密歇根州，底特律：韦恩州立大学出版社，2006 年，第 20 页；第 202 页；第 208—212 页。

3 主导命题

要点 🔑

- 瓦尔特·本雅明在《机械复制时代的艺术作品》中详细分析机械复制 * 带来的政治后果。

- 《机械复制时代的艺术作品》基于马克思主义批评观，驳斥艺术具有自律性的普遍看法。

- 本雅明强调，视艺术为永恒不变的观点纯属理想化，容易被操控，以压制改革。

核心问题

20 世纪前几十年里，机械复制的进程在哪些方面改变艺术作品的生产和接受？这些变化产生了什么政治后果？

在这一政治变革时期，当法西斯主义成为公众和学界论辩的焦点之际，本雅明在《机械复制时代的艺术作品》中探究的议题却从未有人谈及。因此，他的这篇论著颇具独创性。为了解答这些议题，本雅明试图通过考察他所谓艺术作品的"灵晕"与技术和历史语境之间的关系，来分析"灵晕"的变化状态。他认为，"在机械复制时代凋萎的东西正是艺术作品的'灵晕'"。[1]

虽然本雅明并未明确定义何为"灵晕"，但他在文中清晰指出，这个概念与艺术在历史上和宗教或皇室仪规的关联密不可分（本雅明称其为"膜拜"价值），亦同伟大的艺术作品具有原真性和自律性这一传统观点息息相关。艺术作品存在于特定情境，有其独特的在场性，人们从四面八方前来观赏。而当它复制于书本或翻印成明信片时，这种特殊意义便遭到消解。机械复制导致艺术作品被擅用——钉在卧室墙面、寄给远房亲戚，甚至将其与咖啡广告并置。这种可复制性能产生民主化效果。不仅如此，新技术还催生出新的艺术形式，如电影和摄影，不再需要独一无二的原初物象。不存在"原初的"电影胶片或相片：所有复制品都一模一样。

> "曾经，人们竭力思索能否将摄影术视作一门艺术，结果徒劳无功。最关键的问题——摄影术的发明是否已经改变艺术的全部本质——还未被提及。"
>
> ——瓦尔特·本雅明：《机械复制时代的艺术作品》

参与者

本雅明这篇论著围绕两组普遍的共识展开探讨。首先是传统艺术批评理论中仍占主导地位的观点，即认为艺术作品是具有自律性的物象，并处于孤立空间之中，与日常的现实物质世界毫无关联，本雅明对此予以驳斥。这种物象正因其独特性而被视为艺术作品，不仅能够反映其创作背景，亦能**超越**其历史语境。它看似蕴含某些永恒不变的价值核心，可以流芳千古，这也正体现出它的原真性和独特性。本雅明称之为艺术作品的"灵晕"，使其在后世被观赏和接受的过程中显得独一无二。

再者是西方马克思主义——这一术语的提出者是哲学家莫里斯·梅洛-庞蒂*，泛指西欧和中欧地区的各种马克思主义思潮。本雅明的论著对资本主义和艺术史提出激烈批判，因为他发现，那些与传统艺术观相关的概念，成为资本主义和法西斯主义的帮凶。他的研究视角聚焦于文化生产，而非艺术的形式技艺，与他在文中引述的其他思想家的观点有许多共通之处。

当代论战

本雅明在文中指出，传统艺术史秉持的艺术观纯属理想化，轻易就被利用，以维持社会不公的现状并使其合理化。若执意将艺术从其历史语境中分离，将导致一种更普遍的局面，使占主导地位的文化制约任何挑战现状的企图，且主流文化还得以兼并和消解所有异议。

在法西斯主义兴起的背景下，本雅明的论著揭示出，固守传统艺术观，即认为艺术作品具有原真性、自律性，且永恒不变，将酿成严重的政治后果：因为这正是纳粹政权使其暴力和镇压行为合法化的工具。本雅明认为，这导致政治美学化：政治领袖能够欺骗公众，迫使人们将民族国家视为一件永恒不变且不可变革的艺术作品。本雅明希望改变这种局面，试图通过使艺术政治化的方式，鼓舞大众掀起颠覆性的政治运动。

因此，本雅明试图将艺术研究与更为宏阔的社会文化进程联系起来，考察它对艺术作品生产（如何制成）、接受（如何观赏），以及复制（如何传播）产生的影响。将艺术作品置于更为宽广的历史语境中加以考察，使本雅明得以反思传统艺术观可能导致的严重局限和政治后果。继而，他基于马克思主义文化观，以开创性的视角看待艺术史。不过，许多马克思主义思想家，诸如齐格弗里德·克拉考尔*和西奥多·阿多诺，都将大众文化视为一种分神消遣，最终使公众避免卷入政治纷争，但本雅明则与众不同：他坚信，大众文化具有推动彻底变革的潜力。克拉考尔和阿多诺将新兴媒介视为资本主义剥削的新工具，本雅明却认为新兴媒介能发挥"震颤"作用，将大众动员起来。

---

1. 瓦尔特·本雅明："机械复制时代的艺术作品"，《启迪》，汉娜·阿伦特编，伦敦：皮姆里科出版社，1999 年，第 215 页。

4 作者贡献

要点 🗝━

- 《机械复制时代的艺术作品》中提出的艺术批评理论，旨在反抗法西斯主义，并可用以推动社会变革。

- 新兴媒介的出现和艺术接受模式的更迭，正改变着公众看待艺术和传播的方式。

- 本雅明的观点独树一帜。他往往运用类似拼贴画 * 和蒙太奇 * 的技巧，在引用文献时重新阐述他人的话语。

作者目标

瓦尔特·本雅明写作《机械复制时代的艺术作品》一文，旨在与法西斯主义抗争，或者至少是对现代艺术抱以一种批评和反思的姿态，认为其不应与法西斯主义为伍。纳粹政权在德国实施法西斯主义政策，压制公民自由，并针对特定种族实施迫害——主要是规模庞大而多元的犹太社群，本雅明一家也未能幸免。在此背景下，对这部作品的吁求显得愈发迫切。本雅明通过分析生产、接受和复制等新技术时代的艺术作品，试图探讨：西方资本主义政权占据主导地位，加之右翼极端势力兴起，致使大众被异化并受压迫；那么，新技术催生的艺术形式将如何反映这些大众的利益诉求？或许是通过彻底革命，抑或需要开辟更民主的途径，对艺术和文化展开整体性思考。

本雅明有关大众文化（主要指电影，也包括摄影、杂志和流行小说等）具有革命潜力的乐观看法，与他的马克思主义同仁截然不同，尤其在当时那些更保守的艺术评论家看来，显得格格不入。那些法兰克福学派的学者认为，大众文化导致消极情绪——使人们成为精神涣散、缺乏批判力的消费者和观赏者，丝毫不关心政治——可以被用来控制公共舆论。保守派艺术评论家则坚信，大众文化扼杀心智和想象力：他们认为，中产阶级读者应当远离那些专供底层人士消费的"垃圾"。那些艺术评论家们更进一步指出，新兴艺术形式削弱他们作为专家的权威性：本雅明就曾写道，"电影技术如同运动技巧一样，凡是目睹其成就的观众，或多或少皆可算作专家。"[1]艺术评论家将这种公平竞争的环境视为威胁。本雅明这篇论著独具匠心，不仅反映在他对可复制性的分析上，亦同样体现在其对未来影响的乐观看法上。

> "在漫长的历史岁月中，人类的感知方式随着整体生存方式的更迭而改变。人类感官知觉的构成方式——感知过程赖以实现的载体——不仅受制于自然环境，也受制于历史条件。"
>
> ——瓦尔特·本雅明：《机械复制时代的艺术作品》

研究方法

本雅明的写作思路与众不同。他将全文分解成十四个"命题*"，或可称作精编短文，并在这些短论中提出一系列观点，不仅回顾艺术复制和艺术作品"灵晕"消逝的历史，还分析摄影和电影的特殊技法特征、观众和媒介的变化关系，以及分神消遣所具有的革命潜力。一系列论断看似各不相同，实则环环相扣。他一方面探讨新兴媒介的特征，另一方面则论述公众与艺术和修辞术*（即信息表达方式）之间的关系转型，由此揭示这两方面的联系。他观点的独创性正体现于此：本雅明认为，正是摄影和电影所具有的特征，使其形式具有非原真性，这将改变公众对于**一切**表演和表达形式的接受模式——不仅包括绘画、音乐和戏剧，还有演讲、游行，以及法西斯主义领袖所擅长的其他公共宣传活动，迫使大众效忠其政权。本雅明指出，新兴媒介将推动整个美学领域（艺术和展览）掀起新的怀疑主义思潮，使得人们能够辨别政治领袖是否在通过营造"景观"来操控公共舆论。因此，在本雅明看来，随着新兴媒介的诞生，传统艺术作品的权威性逐渐消解；同时，公众接受艺术作品的模式发生转变。这些将赋予人们新的抗争手段，来反击法西斯主义。这一观点可谓独树一帜。

时代贡献

《机械复制时代的艺术作品》是一篇独具匠心的论著，但字里行间也能寻得其他众多思想家的痕迹。这尤其体现在全文最广为人知的第一句话，"当马克思着手批判资本主义生产方式*的时候，这种生产方式尚处于初级阶段。"[2] 此外，还有许多作家、哲学家和评论家的观点在文中亦有引述。本雅明在这篇论著中引用马克思和其他相关文献的目的，与他的其他著作一样，都是为了将其观点置于马克思主义话语立场中，并旨在回应当时艺术和文学批评领域存在的论争。例如，这篇论著的卷首语（即正文之前的引言）出自法国诗人、散文家保罗·瓦雷里*（1871—1945）的作品《无处不在的征服》（1928）*。文中，瓦雷里对新兴技术在文化领域产生的潜在影响展开了推测。[3]

本雅明还在后文中引用了这部作品的另一段话："我们几乎不费吹灰之力，就能将水、煤气和电从遥远的地方引进住宅而为我们服务。与之相似，将来也会有视听影像提供给我们，为此只需做个简单动作，或许就是个手势，便能使其出现和消失。"[4] 然而，瓦雷里这段话原本意指技术正潜移默化地飞速改变人们的生活。但本雅明引用这段话则是为了佐证自己的观点，即传统艺术形式亟待新兴技术的变革。

这正体现本雅明的写作特色，他总是赋予其他作家的文字以新的含义。他之所以引用文献，从不是为了借用他人的看法，而是为了重新阐述他们的话语，最终支撑他自己与众不同的观点。这种写作方式与拼贴画和电影文学蒙太奇手法颇为相似。本雅明对这两种技巧很感兴趣。这两种技巧都是先将不同来源的材料片段（往往毫不相干）并置，继而赋予其新的含义。如今，读者在阅读这些脱离语境的引文时，或许会产生截然不同的看法——例如，瓦雷里的那段引文似乎预言了互联网的诞生，这着实令人诧异。

---

1. 瓦尔特·本雅明："机械复制时代的艺术作品"，《启迪》，汉娜·阿伦特编，伦敦：皮姆里科出版社，1999 年，第 225 页。
2. 本雅明："机械复制时代的艺术作品"，第 211 页。
3. 保罗·瓦雷里："无处不在的征服"（1928 年），《美学》，拉尔夫·曼海姆译，纽约：万神殿图书公司，1964 年，第 226 页，转引于"机械复制时代的艺术作品"，第 211 页。

第二部分：学术思想

5 思想主脉

要点 ⚷

- 《机械复制时代的艺术作品》关注的主要问题是：新兴技术赋予艺术作品的可复制性，将产生何种社会影响？

- 本雅明认为，可复制性能拓展艺术作品的受众范围，继而得以挑战传统艺术批评理论，并掀起政治变革。

- 本雅明始终坚信，艺术批评不应墨守成规，而他碎片式的写作风格正与之相契合。

核心主题

本雅明这篇论著的主要论题是探讨艺术作品、复制技术和政治变革之间的关系。传统观点认为，艺术作品具有自律性、原真性，其价值永恒不变，沉浸在"灵晕"包围中。然而，与之相悖的是，新兴技术使艺术作品具有可复制性。本雅明认为，随着图像的大众化传播，艺术作品的"灵晕"逐渐消逝。艺术作品走向民主化，变得更为平易近人，不再成为宗教和皇室的特权。

本雅明将这一观点与漫长的历史转型联系在一起，即艺术作品从仪式器物——依托魔法和宗教，抑或作为美的化身供人沉思——转变为：政治工具。基于这一历史视角，本雅明还勾勒出与之相关的变化，即艺术作品的膜拜价值（作为仪式器物）转变为展示价值（作为展览对象）。他指出，现代艺术不仅能够操控大众使之屈从，亦能使大众获得自由解放。

对本雅明而言，电影和摄影的诞生，影响着我们感知和体验世界的方式，并赋予我们挑战政权压迫的能力。其原因在于，电影明显缺乏原真性——根本无法辨别一部电影使用的是"原初"胶片还是其复制品。电影媒介本身即是为复制和传播而生——遂使观众更谨慎对待其他虚假的展示形式，例如，极权主义领袖往往通过游行活动，蒙骗公众使之屈服其政权（本雅明称为"政治美学化"）。据本雅明所论，电影和传统艺术形式的观赏方式大相径庭，这会影响观众对其他展示形式的体验，包括意识形态宣传："公众成为评判者，却无需专心致志。"[1]

> "一旦艺术生产的原真性标准失灵，艺术的整个功能便彻底颠覆。它不再以仪式为依托，而是基于另一种实践——那就是政治。"
>
> —— 瓦尔特·本雅明：《机械复制时代的艺术作品》

思想探究

在命题一和命题二中，本雅明探讨了"灵晕"的概念。既然一切艺术都具有可复制性，那么一件绘画作品的摹本就不会损害原作的权威性，因为它很容易就被判定为赝品。可是，机械复制品却独立于原作：首先，机械复制能突出展现原作中不易被捕捉的细节；其次，它能将原作传播至任何地方。[2]

这些特征不仅导致灵晕的衰减，还不可避免地改变人们感知周围世界的方式。事实上，本雅明认为，电影将改变"人类的整体生存方式"[3]，因此它是 20 世纪最卓尔不群的"人类感知模式"。[4]电影最具影响力的特征，就是其大众化的接受方式（人们集体观看电影，使电影工业能够获得远比画廊展览更广泛的受众）。而且，电影还使观众能以更聚焦、更清晰的视角，打量周围的世界。

命题四和命题五介绍"为艺术而艺术"*的过时观点：这一概念是指艺术应当受到尊重，而非批判，艺术应当拥有高于观赏者的地位。本雅明认为，这是意指保留艺术的膜拜功能。本雅明提出，可复制性赋予艺术作品以政治内涵。例如，20世纪初，尤金·阿特盖*的摄影作品被刊登在杂志和报刊文章中，成为"历史现场的标准证据"，从而"获得政治意义"。[5]

本雅明同时指出，电影和报刊一样，需要观众投身其中，这导致"作者和公众之间的区分……逐渐失去其基本特征"。[6]确切而言："如今，每个人都可提出被拍成电影的要求；"[7]同样，"但凡是有工作、有收入的欧洲人，现在原则上都有机会在某个地方发表工作心得。"[8]然而，本雅明在此所关心的，并非摄影或电影是否具有传播改革思想的潜力(他提到,这一想法可以为出版商或生产商所用)，而是"对传统艺术观念展开革命性批判"的潜力。[9]虽然这些新兴艺术形式或许并不能促成社会变革，但它们有助于革新对艺术的过时看法——这些看法蕴含着风险，导致人们始终受制于社会结构的压迫。

最后，也是最具争议性的观点是，本雅明提出，新兴媒介使观赏者的注意力和接收信息的能力减弱，这应当被视为优点。分神消遣*是抵抗大众文化诸种诱惑(广告牌、商店橱窗、小报花边新闻)的途径，能够维持个人有限的精力，去关注重要信息和政治行动。电影作为一种分神消遣活动，可以抵御资本主义文化对个体精神力量的压迫，故而应被视为一种长期的手段。

语言表达

本雅明的挚友兼合作者西奥多·阿多诺曾写道，本雅明善作论说文，在形式上分解成前后呼应的多个论题，最终构成一篇连贯的论作，可谓"无与伦比的大师"。[10] 阿多诺更进一步解释说，在这样的文章里，思想"并非单向发展；各个灵感迸发的契机像地毯纹理一样相互交织。思想的多产程度取决于这种织物的密度"。[11] 然而，阿多诺也评论道，本雅明"有关'碎片化'的哲学思想，自身亦显得残缺不全，"这正是他所青睐的写作方式造成的缺陷。在阿多诺看来，这种写作方式"无法脱离其内容而存在"。[12]

这种碎片式写作充分体现在《机械复制时代的艺术作品》中。全文共分为十四个独立的命题，并加上序言和后记——本雅明通过这种方式，来避免读者刻意区分行文形式（文学特征）和内容（信息内涵）。这一点非常重要，因为本雅明自己就认为，将形式与内容区别对待，不仅是过时的做法，也存在政治上的隐患：两者必须联系在一起，共同加以考察。如此有违正统的文本风格，恰好与本雅明离经叛道的论辩相契合，即并非提出一个单一、连贯且包罗万象的观点，而是抛出一系列关系松散的概念。这种写作风格可以避免读者妄下结论，这也正是为何本雅明的著作至今仍能引起热议的原因。

---

1. 瓦尔特·本雅明："机械复制时代的艺术作品"，《启迪》，汉娜·阿伦特编，伦敦：皮姆里科出版社，1999 年，第 234 页。
2. 本雅明："机械复制时代的艺术作品"，第 214 页。
3. 本雅明："机械复制时代的艺术作品"，第 216 页。
4. 本雅明："机械复制时代的艺术作品"，第 216 页。

5. 本雅明："机械复制时代的艺术作品"，第 220 页。

6. 本雅明："机械复制时代的艺术作品"，第 225 页。

7. 本雅明："机械复制时代的艺术作品"，第 225 页。

8. 本雅明："机械复制时代的艺术作品"，第 225 页。

9. 本雅明："机械复制时代的艺术作品"，第 224 页。

10. 西奥多·W·阿多诺："作为形式的散文"，《文学笔记:第一辑》，谢利·韦伯·尼科尔森，纽约：哥伦比亚大学出版社，1991 年，第 3—23 页（第 13 页）。

11. 阿多诺："作为形式的散文"，第 13 页。

12. 西奥多·W. 阿多诺："瓦尔特·本雅明传略"，《棱镜》，塞缪尔和谢利·韦伯译，马萨诸塞州，坎布里奇：麻省理工学院出版社，1988 年，第 227—242 页（第 239 页）。

6 思想支脉

要点 ⚿

- 《机械复制时代的艺术作品》还从更为宽泛的视角探讨摄影术、电影以及技术革新如何影响我们看待周围的世界。

- 本雅明认为，摄像机镜头改变演员和观众的关系，并揭示这个世界被遮蔽的侧面。他指出，电影能迅速引人入胜，产生身临其境之感，人们无需专心致志便可体验其中。

- 虽然本雅明这篇论著旨在展开政治批评，却往往被视作一篇艺术评论。因此，他的诸多核心论点遭到忽视。

其他思想

虽然《机械复制时代的艺术作品》探讨的核心论题是艺术批评如何可被用以反抗法西斯主义，但文中还着重分析了另一个论题，即电影和摄影的特殊技巧如何彻底颠覆我们看待周围世界的方式——并反思技术本身。当本雅明阐述灵晕、艺术政治化和政治美学化等概念时，这些论点尽管是次要的，但依然有助于充分领会这篇论著和他的其他作品。其中值得一提的包括：他考察发现，摄像机能够协调演员和观众的传统关系；他分析指出，摄像机可以揭示这个世界被遮蔽的侧面；他还坚信，相较于实验绘画，集体观赏使观众更容易接受实验电影，因为前者的观众是独自参观的中产阶级，仍受制于艺术评论家的权威。

在命题七中，本雅明提到，摄影术诞生之际，评论家争论不休，"能否将摄影术视作一门艺术？最关键的问题——摄影术的发明是否已经改变艺术的全部本质——还未被提及"。[1] 本雅明便通过这篇论著展开探讨。

> "显然，由画报和新闻纪录片展现的复制品就与肉眼所见的形象不尽相同。后者与独一无二性和永恒性密切相关，而前者则与暂时性和可复制性紧密相连。"
>
> —— 瓦尔特·本雅明:《机械复制时代的艺术作品》

思想探究

本雅明认为，电影通过摄像机镜头改变了演员和观众的传统关系。摄像机通过变换视角或使用特写镜头，对演员的形象和动作实施操纵。而这些表演动作通常是在舞台上拍摄，后来才被合成在电影中：这一切使观众和演员之间产生距离。"观众对于演员的认同，实际是对于摄像机镜头的认同。"[2] 同样，电影演员并非直接面对观众，并不会像舞台演员那样根据观众的反映来调整下一场演出，因而电影演员与观众的关系，更像是货架上的商品与购买者之间的关系。在拍摄过程中，"电影演员（和观众）没有实质接触，如同商品在工厂里生产时并未与市场接触一样"。[3]

然而，与此同时，电影亦能使观众观察诸多细微之处——地理风貌的细节、某个人物的步态，或是水龙头的滴答声——这些细微之处我们一般难以察觉。他将这种突出细节的能力与精神分析学家的技能相提并论。精神分析学*认为，个体生命的组成部分包括有意识的思想和行动，以及成百上千次无意识的冲动、欲望和厌恶之情——之所以无意识，是因为这些情绪发生在潜意识中。正如精神分析学家观察个体意识一样，电影揭示出我们过去没有意识到的世界面貌。电影镜头的减速和加速，能使我们对被拍摄物体产生全新

34

的理解。"摄像机使我们认识何为无意识视觉，犹如精神分析学带我们了解何为无意识冲动。"[4]

同样，电影提供了一种身临其境的体验：在命题十一中，本雅明将画家比作巫师，将摄影师比作外科医生，且将现实比作接受治疗的病体。画家犹如巫师，在病体上方移动双手，并未与之接触，保持着"与病患自然的距离"，而摄影师则像是外科医生，直接切开病体，"深入穿透"其中。[5]

此外，本雅明还将电影与建筑艺术相比较，观众无需凝神专注便有身临其境之感。这一论点与一个更宏大的命题相关，即最先锋的艺术实践和最先进的技术之间存在时间差。本雅明指出，艺术期待变革，未来的技术将使艺术传播得更为广泛，并使之成为主流："正如石版印刷孕育着画报的诞生，摄影技术也预示着有声电影的问世。"[6]出于同样的原因，城市居民对于建筑艺术亦是抱以分神消遣的态度，他们并不会凝神驻足仔细观察，恰如电影观众，他们"成为评判者，却无需专心致志。"[7]

上述论点从侧面呼应本雅明这篇论著的主题思想，阐述技术可复制性对于艺术作品的生产和接受产生何种影响，并揭示其如何广泛形塑现代性体验和感知。

被忽视之处

长期以来，本雅明这篇论著的政治意义鲜有被关注。在不同时期的版本差别更凸显这一事实。由于本雅明在文中引用马克思的文献，并公开支持社会主义，反对法西斯主义，因而出版之初便遭到查禁。然而，即便是这篇论著最通行的英译本——上述引文都得以保留——用本雅明研究专家苏珊·巴克-莫斯[*]的话来说，"至少在美国读者眼中，通常被视作对文化产业彻底走向去政治化*的捍卫"，而非通过大众文化来挑战极权主义*的尝试。[8]莫斯认为，本雅明这篇论著恰是政治美学*的宣言：它反映出任何有关艺术的探讨都与政治息息相关。如果忽视本雅明论述中的政治维度，则无法全面领会这篇论著的要旨。

倘若将本雅明这篇论著视为一份政治宣言，则更容易理解该文与本雅明其他论著之间的关系，诸如《作为生产者的作家》*《历史哲学论纲》*等。这些论著都试图揭示文化生产（这篇论著中是指艺术生产和历史书写）的政治意义。

事实上，本雅明研究和其他学科领域的学者早已对这篇论著展开了深入研读和探究，尽管其政治意涵遭到忽视。学者们迫切想将文中的观点用于对新兴技术的探讨。甚至可以说——如同莫斯在她先前那段话中所述——本雅明这篇论著已被混用，往往曲解了本意。

---

1. 瓦尔特·本雅明："机械复制时代的艺术作品"，《启迪》，汉娜·阿伦特编，伦敦：皮姆里科出版社，1999年，第220页。

2. 本雅明："机械复制时代的艺术作品"，第222页。

3. 本雅明："机械复制时代的艺术作品"，第224页。

4. 本雅明："机械复制时代的艺术作品"，第230页。

5. 本雅明："机械复制时代的艺术作品"，第227页。

6. 本雅明："机械复制时代的艺术作品"，第213页。

7. 本雅明："机械复制时代的艺术作品"，第234页。

8. 苏珊·巴克－莫斯：“反斯大林主义的艺术：本雅明、肖斯塔科维奇，以及故事的结尾”，国际瓦尔特·本雅明协会第一次全体大会主旨演讲，阿姆斯特丹，1997 年 7 月。正式文稿题为“革命时代：前卫艺术与先锋派”，《本雅明研究》，第 1 辑，海尔格·盖耶－赖恩编，阿姆斯特丹：罗德匹出版社，2002 年，登录日期 2017 年 7 月 13 日，http://susanbuckmorss.info/text/antistalinist-art/。

7 历史成就

要点 🔑

- 《机械复制时代的艺术作品》是一篇颇具影响力的论著，虽然文中有关大众文化和新兴媒介的分析显得过于乐观。

- 本雅明这篇论著的原稿几经修改，有关电影和摄影的地位，以及法西斯主义的兴起等议题，在当时引起纷争。

- 艺术市场最终将艺术作品真迹的"灵晕"商业化，而《机械复制时代的艺术作品》未能预料到这一点。

观点评价

正如本雅明在论著的标题中所暗示，《机械复制时代的艺术作品》不仅探讨艺术作品，还聚焦技术。本雅明在文中追溯现代社会感知方式诸种演变的缘起，继而考察新兴技术和创意实践。出人意料的是，从这个视角而言，这篇论著竟然与当今的数字化时代颇有关联。在这个数字化时代，新兴技术——计算机、互联网、移动电话——彻底改变了我们与外部世界的交互方式（亦在技术层面颠覆艺术家的创作模式）。[1]

然而，本雅明强调电影乃革命性的关键媒介，能够推动文化变革。事实证明，他显然过于乐观，因为电影院现已成为极其反动 * 且程式化的主流场所。他在文中指出，电影明星沉浸在虚构的灵晕之中，使观众和演员之间延续着某种相似的距离感。本雅明希望，可以通过蒙太奇手法（将碎片化的短片剪辑合并来讲述故事）和其他视觉特效，打破这种距离感。可是，这些特效并不能使观众感到震颤。他们仍消极沉思，深陷于似乎永恒不变且不可变革的社会体系中，无法投身更为积极的世界转型之中。[2]

> "有史以来，机械复制第一次使艺术作品从对仪式的寄生和依赖中解放出来。被复制的艺术作品愈发成为专为可复制性而设计的艺术作品。例如，我们可以用一张底片印制任意数量的相片，但若要鉴别何者为'真品'则显得荒唐可笑。"
>
> ——瓦尔特·本雅明:《机械复制时代的艺术作品》

当时的成就

本雅明这篇论著的出版和接受深受紧张的政治时局影响——该文第一稿在出版时有所删改，以免使目标读者产生疏离感。值得注意的是，当社会研究所准备将这篇尚未发表的论著翻译成法语时，正文开篇引用卡尔·马克思著作的语句被编辑悉数删除。[3] 提及"法西斯主义"的表述也被修改成较为含蓄的"极权主义政权。"[4] 经过数次讨论，本雅明很不情愿地接受了编辑的修改，因为他当时处于极度贫困之中。其中一部分原因是，他先前的多个出版渠道已被纳粹政府下令封禁，而他迫切想表达自己的想法：换言之，交由社会研究所出版，是他最后的机会。本书使用的英语文本由该文第三稿翻译而成，有关马克思和法西斯主义等内容均得到保留（本雅明对电影的重要价值曾做过篇幅更长的论述，旨在从文化和政治的角度分析艺术和技术，而这段讨论亦收录在该版中）。

本雅明激进的文笔在编辑过程中被弱化，反映出社会研究所竭力避免在这个接纳他们的新国家引起非议（1934 年，研究所为逃避纳粹迫害而迁往纽约）。[5] 这些修改也证明本雅明与研究所领导之间存在诸多重要分歧。尤为鲜明的是，阿多诺认为，本雅明在与贝托尔特·布莱希特相识之后，产生了不切实际的乐观想法，损害了这篇论著的观点独创性。[6] 据阿多诺所言，本雅明深受布莱希特的影响，继而抱以一种过于乐观的看法，想当然地认为可复制性技术孕育着革命潜力，并未从理论上展开更为系统的分析。[7] 于是，研究所发表的版本将阿多诺对于大众文化更具批判性的看法，与本雅明激进乐观主义的思想融合在一起。

局限性

值得商榷的是，本雅明将可机械复制的艺术作品聚焦在两种特定形式上——摄影和电影——这与当时所处的历史发展阶段有关，使其应用价值受到局限。现如今，摄影和电影等媒介正逐渐与其他技术紧密结合，因而相较于本雅明发表这篇论著的时代，文中的部分观点已经缺乏足够的说服力。

还需要指出的是，本雅明预测新兴技术带来的变革实际并未发生。本雅明所谓蒙太奇、特写镜头和特效等手法制造的"震颤"效果，早已成为主流电影的基本特征，观众对此已经习以为常。本雅明将电影特效与达达主义和超现实主义通过实验艺术作品来实现的震颤效果相提并论。后者的所作所为旨在避免像传统绘画作品那样发人深省，引起学究式的批评。[8] 达达主义者为了"激怒公众"，而将作品置于"丑闻中心"[9]——最著名的案例便是马塞尔·杜尚署名并展出的那个便池。达达主义者们无意迎合观众，"其作品是宣泄怒火的武器。就像一枚导弹击中观众，一切皆是突如其来"。[10] 现在，超现实主义和和达达主义已被视为艺术史的组成部分，相关作品被陈列在各大著名美术馆里。与之相反，本雅明眼中具有革命性的视觉作品，如今却是随处可见。同样，本雅明认为，在机械复制时代，萦绕在艺术作品周围的灵晕逐渐消逝。可是，许多热门艺术展览在全球各地巡回展出，吸引着数百万参观者。本雅明的观点似乎并不能对此予以解释。这些展览将"真迹"作为独家卖点，大获成功。

1. 安卡·普斯卡编：《瓦尔特·本雅明与变革的美学》，纽约、贝辛斯托克：帕尔格雷夫·麦克米伦出版公司，2010 年，具体参见：康斯坦丁·瓦西里欧："数字化时代艺术的灵晕"，第 158—170 页。

2. 苏珊·桑塔格："电影的衰落"，《纽约时报》，1996 年 2 月 25 日，登录日期 2017 年 7 月 13 日，http://www.nytimes.com/books/00/03/12/specials/sontag-cinema.html。

3. 伊斯特·莱斯利："屈服投降时代的艺术作品"，《瓦尔特·本雅明：克服因循守旧》，伦敦：雷克申出版社，2000 年，第 130—167 页。

4. 莱斯利："屈服投降时代的艺术作品"，第 131 页。

5. 莱斯利："屈服投降时代的艺术作品"，第 130 和 131 页。

6. 西奥多·W. 阿多诺和瓦尔特·本雅明：《通信全集：1928—1940 年》，尼古拉斯·沃克译，剑桥：政体出版社，1999 年，第 127—134 页（第 130 页）。

7. 阿多诺和本雅明：《通信全集》，第 130 页。

8. 瓦尔特·本雅明："机械复制时代的艺术作品"，《启迪》，汉娜·阿伦特编，伦敦：皮姆里科出版社，1999 年，第 231 页。

9. 本雅明："机械复制时代的艺术作品"，第 231 页。

10. 本雅明："机械复制时代的艺术作品"，第 231 页。

8 著作地位

要点 ⌚

- 《机械复制时代的艺术作品》的最终版是本雅明创作生涯的倒数第二部作品，出版于他扑朔迷离的自杀事件前一年。

- 《机械复制时代的艺术作品》中的诸多思想观点，基于本雅明在其先前论著中有关摄影、文学和巴黎拱廊街的探讨。

- 随着本雅明之前未发表的作品相继问世，他这篇代表作便逐渐被边缘化了。

定位

《机械复制时代的艺术作品》第三稿，也即最终稿，是本雅明的遗作之一，完成于 1939 年——正是他扑朔迷离的自杀事件前一年。这篇论著的核心内容围绕艺术、摄影和电影生产的境况展开，并关注艺术在政治领域的派生影响；然而，与之相关的论题实则贯穿本雅明的整个创作生涯。特别值得一提的是，这篇论著其实是基于他先前的文章——《摄影小史》，文中他探讨了摄影所引发的视觉模式变化。他指出，"灵晕的消逝标志着某种知觉的现身——这种对于事物相似性的感知能力已经如此成熟，即便是原本独一无二的事物，也经由复制而失去独特性。"[2] 他还提出"视觉无意识"[3]这一概念，与《机械复制时代的艺术作品》中的对应表述在形式上略有差别。在后一篇论著中，他指出，特写和慢镜头等摄影摄像技术展现出"物象崭新的结构组成"，犹如精神分析学家揭开无意识冲动的奥秘一样。[4]

在《作为生产者的作家》（1934）一文中，亦能找到与《机械复制时代的艺术作品》的诸多相似之处。本雅明写道，在资本主义社会，出版业天生就与阶级对立息息相关。[5] 作家总是有意无意地秉持某种立场。本雅明呼吁作家与劳动阶层（无产阶级）站在一起，通过内容创作或形式创新，与资产阶级生产方式内在的法西斯主义倾向作抗争。作家们不应将自己视为作品的提供者，以迎合现有的文学形式划分，而应作为生产者去创造全新的文学形式。然而，尽管《作为生产者的作家》所表达的主题思想与《机械复制时代的艺术作品》极为相似（这里主要指印刷而非摄影／电影），但由于文章采用马克思主义强硬派的视角，因而显得过于简单笼统。

> "一切知识都存在于不断阐释之中。"
> —— 瓦尔特·本雅明：《瓦尔特·本雅明书信集（1910—1940）》

整合

本雅明在《机械复制时代的艺术作品》中非常关注艺术生产背后的物质条件，这与《拱廊街计划》的主题相契合，后者是他生命最后十三年里一直在撰写的著作。这一写作计划围绕 19 世纪早期巴黎拱廊（购物街）的建筑形式展开，本雅明认为这是资本主义的幻象。作为曾经的商业中心，这些拱廊街在 19 世纪末被百货公司弃用。本雅明发现，这些空置废弃的拱廊空间，是一种文化象征，昭示着：即便今日奉若至宝，明日亦将弃如敝屣。

《机械复制时代的艺术作品》还与本雅明另一篇写于同时期的论著《讲故事的人》有所关联。后者探讨的论题是，随着印刷复制技术的兴起，讲故事的技艺为何日渐式微。[7]

最后，《机械复制时代的艺术作品》对分神消遣的推崇，亦与本雅明的其他作品产生共鸣。在20世纪第二个十年里，本雅明一直在翻译法国诗人夏尔·波德莱尔的作品。波德莱尔在《现代生活的画家》（1863）*中写道，现代都市生活需要一种全新的呈现方式，来反映资本主义城市流变的特征。对波德莱尔而言，"flâneur"（漫游者*）的形象展现出现代诗人所必须拥有的特质：保持开放的态度去吸纳（描写）城市中诸多令人震颤和诱惑的事物。本雅明则认为，这种想法在20世纪已变得不合时宜：因为资本主义消费文化早已将"漫游者"扼杀在摇篮里。时值20世纪，资本主义不断迫使公众投身于消费和交易的进程之中，使心不在焉的漫游行为变得不切实际。因此，本雅明在《机械复制时代的艺术作品》中，将电影视为一种全新的替代方式，来营构类似19世纪"漫游者"所享有的分神消遣状态：分神消遣并非意味着消极享乐，而是沉着冷静地保持疏离。[8]

意义

尽管《机械复制时代的艺术作品》所提出的观点独树一帜，但其离经叛道的写作方式则是本雅明一贯的风格。他总是能将众多碎片化的思想融汇在一起，内容涵盖艺术、建筑、电影、摄影、历史、文学、哲学和政治等看似独立的学科。本雅明在他的论作中，把这些不同领域的思想片段组合起来，从而形成极富创见的视角，来探讨艺术与政治、文化生产以及技术复制等话题。

本雅明是20世纪最具影响力的思想家之一，而《机械复制时代的艺术作品》则是他最广为人知的著作，可谓"改变游戏规则"的代表作（尽管他逝世多年以后，这一认可才姗姗来迟）。自20世纪 60 年代末首个英译本出版以来，这篇论著对很多人来说是了解本雅明文献的重要入门资料，也是研究 20 世纪文化和现代性的重要参照标准。

然而，近年来，尽管本雅明作为评论家和哲学家依然引人瞩目，但有关这篇论著的探讨却有所降温。这很大程度上是因为学者们的研究兴趣逐渐转移至他的其他作品——其中最赫赫有名的便是《历史哲学论纲》。[9] 这是本雅明最后一篇完稿的论著，文中对历史主义 *（探讨历史语境下意义的归属问题，并透过时代背景分析历史现象）展开批评。

当代知识评论界对《机械复制时代的艺术作品》的关注度降低，还有一个原因就是，自本雅明逝世以来，他的其他著作都有译本陆续问世。[10] 最值得一提的是，本雅明当年在巴黎最后的寓所被盖世太保查抄的作品手稿，直至 1996 年才收藏至位于柏林的瓦尔特·本雅明档案馆。[11] 而伊斯特·莱斯利 *，以及霍华德·艾兰 * 和迈克尔·W. 汤普森先后于 2007 年和 2013 年出版的两部本雅明传记，亦为本雅明研究提供了新的思路。[12] 在这些作品的启发下，本雅明较为冷门的著作相继得到评论界的重视，同时其译本也不断推陈出新。因此，虽然《机械复制时代的艺术作品》仍属扛鼎之作，但它或许早已完成其原有的使命——揭开本雅明复杂思想的面纱，使其在永无止境的阐释之中继续流传于世。

1. 瓦尔特·本雅明："摄影小史"，《〈单向街〉与其他作品》，埃德蒙·杰普科特和金斯利·肖特译，伦敦：维尔索出版社，1999年，第240—257页。

2. 本雅明："摄影小史"，第250页。

3. 本雅明："摄影小史"，第243页。

4. 瓦尔特·本雅明："机械复制时代的艺术作品"，《启迪》，汉娜·阿伦特编，伦敦：皮姆里科出版社，1999年，第229页。

5. 瓦尔特·本雅明："作为生产者的作家"，《理解布莱希特》，安娜·博斯托克译，伦敦：维尔索出版社，2003年，第85—103页。

6. 瓦尔特·本雅明：《拱廊街计划》，霍华德·艾兰和凯文·麦克洛林编译，马萨诸塞州，坎布里奇：贝尔纳普出版社／哈佛大学出版社，1999年。

7. 瓦尔特·本雅明："说故事的人"，《启迪》，哈里·佐恩译，伦敦：丰塔纳出版社，1982年，第83—109页。

8. 本雅明："机械复制时代的艺术作品"，第233—234页。

9. 瓦尔特·本雅明："历史哲学论纲"，《启迪》，哈里·佐恩译，伦敦：丰塔纳出版社，1982年，第255—266页。这篇文稿的别名是《论历史概念》。

10. 罗尔夫·J. 戈贝尔："简介：本雅明其人"，《瓦尔特·本雅明论著指南》，罗尔夫·戈贝尔编，伦敦：卡姆登书屋，2009年，第2页。

11. 戈贝尔："简介：本雅明其人"，第2页。

12. 伊斯特·莱斯利：《瓦尔特·本雅明》，伦敦：雷克申出版社，2007年；霍华德·艾兰和迈克尔·W. 詹宁斯：《瓦尔特·本雅明：批判的一生》，马萨诸塞州，坎布里奇：贝尔纳普出版社／哈佛大学出版社，2013年。

第三部分：学术影响

9 最初反响

要点 ⌚

- 针对《机械复制时代的艺术作品》的第一篇评论文章发表于这篇论著出版之前，其作者是社会研究所的领袖人物。
- 本雅明与西奥多·阿多诺保持着长期的书信往来，他在信中对这位领袖人物给予的批评作出了回应。
- 尽管《机械复制时代的艺术作品》的部分观点存在缺陷，但文章本身仍是研究 20 世纪艺术、技术和政治的必读之作。

批评

当《机械复制时代的艺术作品》于 1936 年在社会研究所的期刊上初次发表之际（当时是法语译本），一切没能如本雅明所愿，人们并未因此而开始热议美学与政治的关系。[1] 直到将近二十年以后，这篇论著在德国——本雅明的祖国重新发表，以及三十多年后的 1968 年，首个英译本问世，评论界才突然对本雅明的著作产生浓厚兴趣。[2]

第一篇评论文章早在这篇论著正式出版之前就已问世了，作者其实就是社会研究所的那群学者，他们受到委托发表本雅明的这篇论著。本雅明与研究所保持着若即若离的关系。其中，阿多诺曾就这篇论著的优点和不足，与本雅明展开过一场重要讨论。[3]

这场讨论的内容可参见本雅明与阿多诺的书信往来——尤其是阿多诺于 1936 年 3 月在一封回信中所做的论述。[4] 信中，阿多诺批评本雅明对电影拥有革命潜力的看法过于乐观："倘若任何事物都具有类似灵晕的特征，那么电影所体现的这种特征，恰恰是最不足为信的。"[5] 阿多诺表示，以为观看一部默片就"（能够）让一个反动分子转变为先锋派 *"的想法"纯属痴人说梦"。[6] 在他看来，"电影观众捧腹大笑根本毫无益处，亦和革命无关。"[7] 他对本雅明的分神消遣理论也深表怀疑，"假设在一个共产主义社会，人们很可能再也不必为工作辛苦奔波，也不会因加班而昏昏欲睡，这样的话根本就不需要分神消遣。"[8]

阿多诺还指出，电影"几乎不会"像本雅明设想的那样，利用视觉特效来充分展现其革命潜力。他写道，绝大多数电影都只是在试图复制现实。[9] 不过，他的确赞同本雅明对达达主义者震颤技巧的分析，即达达主义者热衷于制造电影里那种震慑人心的效果。[10] 阿多诺的这些批评观点，其实也源自他本人对本雅明其他著作的偏见——他在另一封信中明确坦言："我认为你有关'拱廊街'的探讨不仅是你个人哲学思想的核心内容，也是一个具有决定意义的哲学术语，亟需现在予以表达。"[11]

> "（阿多诺）问道，哪种艺术能更充分揭示我们身处的野蛮环境？既有高雅艺术，亦有通俗艺术。高雅如卡夫卡和勋伯格，他们的文艺作品以技巧取胜，但毫无灵晕，粗鄙不堪，不曾使人有愉悦之感；通俗如迪士尼、卓别林，以及庸俗艺术，个个身披圣痕，一副改革的面貌——米奇（米老鼠）施展魔法，将社会转型的紧迫性一笔勾销。"
> ——伊斯特·莱斯利：《好莱坞平地：动画、批判理论和先锋派》

回应

虽然本雅明认为阿多诺的评论和批评极富建设性，但当他写作第三稿时还是决定坚持自己的立场。事实上，他甚至还删除了第二稿中添加的一段论述——米老鼠动画中的法西斯式暴力，这段论述曾启发阿多诺在《文化工业》一文中对迪士尼展开批判。[12] 不过，为了消除阿多诺的疑虑，他为这篇论著补充了大量脚注。正如著名的本雅明研究专家伊斯特·莱斯利所言，这些注释透露出本雅明纠结矛盾的心态——电影究竟能使大众获得自由解放，还是成为实施压迫的工具。[13] 例如，在脚注七中，本雅明解释道，有声电影的发展有助于克服语言障碍，促进国际传播，却也为法西斯主义服务，满足其民族主义的利益追求（法西斯主义认为观赏外国艺术作品都是叛国行为）。他认为："从外向内看，有声电影被用以强化国家利益，而从内向外看，它使电影生产较以往变得更国际化。"[14]

莱斯利还写道，本雅明这篇论著的后记里"表现得不再那么乐观——技术时代艺术所拥有的全部潜力，在科技神秘主义和国家社会主义者的阶级暴力面前，都消失得无影无踪"。[15] 按照她的解释，本雅明在文章最后指出，"法西斯主义者竭力呈现大众社会的镜像，却无任何实质内容。"他们对大众形象的再现经过精心布置（换言之，将其拍成电影），而并非"以任何富有政治意义的手段呈现（他们）"。[16] 本雅明在此弱化了先前命题中所表现的乐观态度，以此作为对阿多诺担忧的回应。

冲突与共识

由于本雅明刚完成最终稿不久便自杀身亡，他与阿多诺之间的分歧并未得到彻底解决——事实上，在此后的数十年间，学者们依然对此争论不休。此外，虽然这篇论著刚发表时反响平平——未能如本雅明所愿，但现在它已被奉为政治美学领域极具开拓性的文献——政治美学这门学科是由本雅明、阿多诺、霍克海默，以及其他几位法兰克福学派的学者共同创立，主要研究美及其艺术再现在政治语境下所扮演的角色。

自 1968 年英译本问世以来，本雅明这篇论著在 20 世纪 70 年代的英语世界引起巨大轰动。这反映出当时学界的研究焦点已发生变化。本雅明认为，大众文化与"高雅文化"*一样具有研究价值，并且在分析过程中不应秉持全然消极的态度。这些观点后来促进了文学研究和社会科学的发展。例如，文化研究这门学科就和本雅明的作品一样，值得学界重视。文化研究的诞生正是基于这样的认识，即一切文化现象，并非都来自于或服务于上流社会。纵观二战以来商业电影的发展史，尽管本雅明当年深具革命情怀的愿景已显过时，但这篇论著细致入微的论述，仍无愧于成为 20 世纪 30 年代思想批评领域的经典之作，对电影理论和文化研究的发展，发挥着至关重要的推动作用。[17]本雅明指出，在资本主义社会，技术对艺术和文化具有长期影响——虽然文中的相关分析可能并不正确，但他试图阐释这些现象的先锋之举，依然颇具意义。

1. 伊斯特·莱斯利："革命潜力与瓦尔特·本雅明：战后接受史"，《当代马克思主义批评指南》，格利高里·艾力奥特和雅克·比岱编，莱顿：博睿学术出版社，2007 年，第 549—566 页。
2. 莱斯利："革命潜力与瓦尔特·本雅明"，第 549—566 页。
3. 西奥多·W.阿多诺和本雅明：《通信全集：1928—1940 年》，尼古拉斯·沃克译，剑桥：政体出版社，1999 年，第 127—134 页。

4. 阿多诺和本雅明：《通信全集》，第 127—134 页（第 130 页）。

5. 阿多诺和本雅明：《通信全集》，第 132 页。

6. 阿多诺和本雅明：《通信全集》，第 130 页。

7. 阿多诺和本雅明：《通信全集》，第 130 页。

8. 阿多诺和本雅明：《通信全集》，第 130 页。

9. 阿多诺和本雅明：《通信全集》，第 131 页。

10. 阿多诺和本雅明：《通信全集》，第 133 页。

11. 阿多诺和本雅明：《通信全集》，第 85 页。

12. 伊斯特·莱斯利：《好莱坞平地：动画、批判理论和先锋派》，伦敦：维尔索出版社，2002 年，第 117—118 页。本雅明有关迪士尼的探讨参见：瓦尔特·本雅明：《技术可复制时代的艺术作品与其他有关媒介研究的作品》，迈克尔·W. 詹宁斯、布里吉德·多尔蒂和托马斯·Y. 列文编，马萨诸塞州，坎布里奇：贝尔纳普出版社，2008 年，第 318—338 页。

13. 莱斯利：《好莱坞平地》，第 117—118 页。

14. 瓦尔特·本雅明："机械复制时代的艺术作品"，《启迪》，汉娜·阿伦特编，伦敦：皮姆里科出版社，1999 年，第 237 页。

15. 莱斯利：《瓦尔特·本雅明》，伦敦：雷克申出版社，2007 年，第 162 页。

16. 莱斯利：《瓦尔特·本雅明》，第 163 页。

17. 安吉拉·默克罗比："《拱廊街计划》与瓦尔特·本雅明在文化研究中的地位"，《文化研究》第 6 卷，1992 年第 2 期：第 147—169 页。重刊于《文化研究读本》，西蒙·杜林编，伦敦：劳特利奇出版社，1999 年，第 77—96 页。参见：安德鲁·罗宾逊："瓦尔特·本雅明与批评理论"，《停火》，2013 年 4 月 4 日，登录日期 2017 年 7 月 13 日，https://ceasefiremagazine.co.uk/in-theory-benjamin-1/。

10 后续争议

要点 🔑

- 《机械复制时代的艺术作品》的出版史曲折复杂，文稿存在诸多版本，致使英译本的问世相对较晚。

- 本雅明这篇论著是有关政治美学和批判理论的先锋之作，在艺术批评和艺术史研究领域影响深远。

- 学界对本雅明的研究大致分为两类，一类是将其思想应用于大众文化研究，另一类则是从政治维度阐释其作品。

应用与问题

本雅明这篇论著的创作和传播过程历经波折，一方面是作者英年早逝所致，另一方面则是文稿版本和译本众多的缘故。本雅明于1935年在德国完成第一稿。后来，他又写了第二稿，社会研究所对其编辑修订，把原稿中有关马克思的引文悉数删除，并翻译成法语出版。[1] 1939年，本雅明写成最终稿，将先前删除的部分重新补齐。该稿被收入题为《选集》的本雅明论著合集，于1955年在德国出版。[2]

《选集》首个英译本于1968年问世，定名为《启迪》，由德国著名知识分子汉娜·阿伦特编辑，译者是哈利·佐恩。阿伦特还为该书撰写了导论，首发在《纽约客》*杂志上。该译本出版前夕，正值20世纪60年代末学生反抗运动高潮，西德*的高校学生已开始私下传阅本雅明的著作。[3] 当时，大众掀起反建制（如1968年巴黎"五月风暴"*），反对越南战争，反对种族主义、殖民主义*以及反抗社会不公的抗议浪潮。在这一背景下，本雅明的著作再次获得共鸣。

读者对《机械复制时代的艺术作品》的浓厚兴趣，促使本雅明的更多作品被翻译成英语——这些著作有的从未发表，有的只有德语原文。阿多诺编纂的首部本雅明书信集于 1978 年在德国出版，1994 年被翻译成英语。[4] 随后，《拱廊街计划》于 1999 年被翻译成英语，而阿多诺和本雅明书信全集的英译本则于 2001 年问世。[5] 最近，《机械复制时代的艺术作品》的两个新版英译本分别于 2008 年和 2009 年出版：前者以最终稿为原文，译者是 J. A. 安德伍德；后者则以第二稿为原文，译者是迈克尔·詹宁斯，标题为《技术可复制时代的艺术作品》。[6] 这一修订标题更准确贴合本雅明的德文原作，且能更忠实传达本雅明对"Technik"的诠释，既包括"机械"也蕴含"技巧"之义——尽管如此，佐恩 1968 年的译本仍是目前这篇论著最通行的英语文稿。

> "本雅明希望能……发挥……技术的潜力。技术应当被用以推动社会转型，而非巩固混沌不堪的理想国。资产阶级通过保留与技术交织的生产关系，竭力维持理想国的存在。而无产阶级……通过唤起大众的阶级意识，共同实现社会复兴。"
>
> ——伊斯特·莱斯利：《瓦尔特·本雅明：克服因循守旧》

思想流派

本雅明这篇论著影响广泛而深远，直接促成两大思想流派的产生。他与麦克斯·霍克海默、西奥多·阿多诺、埃里希·弗罗姆[*]和赫伯特·马尔库塞[*]共同创立批判理论这一学科。霍克海默在

《传统与批判理论》（1937）* 中指出，倘若某种理论旨在"解放遭受奴役的人类，那么便可以称其具有批判性"。[7]"传统"的自然科学家往往只是尝试解释现象，批判理论学者的研究视角则不同，不仅对现状——尤其是资本主义对权力结构的影响——展开分析，而且还要挑战现状。本雅明这篇论著之所以将机械复制作为论述对象，正是旨在探索反抗主流思想模式的方法，因而被视为批判理论的开山之作。

同样，本雅明与其法兰克福学派的同仁也为政治美学的发展奠定了学术基础。本雅明在《机械复制时代的艺术作品》后记中有个著名论断，"法西斯主义合乎逻辑的结果就是将美学引入政治生活"，而"诉诸政治美学化的一切努力最终归结为一件事：战争"。这便是政治美学的核心概念。此外，政治美学还关注政治思潮和运动如何在文化中获得表达和再现，以此推动意识形态转型，或巩固压迫政权。

纵观艺术史和艺术批评领域，值得一提的是作家、艺术评论家约翰·伯格（1926—2017）。他将本雅明这篇论著中的观点融入其20世纪70年代的电视系列片《观看之道》*。这部专题片随即被改编成一部通俗的艺术史入门读本，目前仍在大学课程中广泛采用。[9]在《观看之道》的第一章，伯格解释道，视艺术作品为独一无二、亘古不变的所谓敬畏之心，实则怀有更大的企图，即巩固主流阶层的地位。当一件艺术作品在技术上具有可复制性时，就会产生另一种颇具威胁性的推论（他称之为"神秘化"）：必须挑战一切。全书最后，伯格将他的想法归功于本雅明这篇论著。[10]

当代研究

概而论之，20 世纪 70 年代以来，学界对本雅明的研究主要有两个分支。首先是美国文化学派。与英国文化学派不同，美国学者自 20 世纪 80 年代中叶起便从去政治化的角度探究大众文化。[11] 多年来，美国文化学派始终将本雅明视为游走在学术边缘的评论家——因为他并未获得学术职位——赞扬他对于日常现象的关注，并认为他推崇电影和摄影的观点值得重视。[12] 美国文化学派很大程度上忽视了本雅明著作中的政治维度。20 世纪 80 年代至 90 年代，在里根*和布什*政府的推动下，新自由主义*意识形态占据上风，而 1991 年苏联*解体亦成为资本主义战胜共产主义*的标志，因而批判理论在美国学界的关注度明显降温，本雅明研究自然也不例外。共产主义瓦解之后，资本主义社会处于经济相对繁荣时期，这似乎意味着反资本主义论著已不再值得研究——美国作家乔纳森·弗兰岑在其 2001 年出版的小说《纠正》中，以讽刺的笔法刻画出这种现状。小说主人公是一位英语教授，他将所有法兰克福学派的著作（包括本雅明的作品）悉数出售换取钱财。[13]

马克思主义文学批评*家特里·伊格尔顿*是第一位从去政治化视角解读本雅明论著的学者。他在 1981 年出版的专著《瓦尔特·本雅明，或走向革命批评》（1981）中公开表示，他写作该书的目的就是要"抢在反对者之前去诠释本雅明。"[14] 本雅明研究的第二个分支正与伊格尔顿的观点遥相呼应，旨在揭示本雅明思想中的激进观念。在这些学者看来，本雅明这篇论著是这位德国犹太裔流亡者最重要的作品，文中第一次明确提出反对资本主义、法西斯主义和战争。我们惟有立足于此，才能通过这篇论著，来反观我们自身所处的文化、历史、政治和社会语境。所以，伊斯特·莱斯利在《瓦尔特·本雅明：克服因循守旧》（2000）里——这是英语世界中最早研究本雅明政治思想的著作之一——指出应当秉持这种视角来整体理解本雅明的作品，即"技术手段加剧……军事暴行。"[15]

1. 伊斯特·莱斯利："屈服投降时代的艺术作品"，《瓦尔特·本雅明：克服因循守旧》，伦敦：雷克申出版社，2000 年，第 131 页。

2. 瓦尔特·本雅明：《选集》，法兰克福：苏尔坎普出版社，1955 年。

3. 伊斯特·莱斯利：《瓦尔特·本雅明》，伦敦：雷克申出版社，2007 年，第 227 页。

4. 瓦尔特·本雅明：《拱廊街计划》，霍华德·艾兰、凯文·麦克洛林编译，马萨诸塞州，坎布里奇：贝尔纳普出版社/哈佛大学出版社，1999 年。

5. 西奥多·W.阿多诺和瓦尔特·本雅明：《通信全集：1928—1940 年》，尼古拉斯·沃克译，剑桥：政体出版社，1999 年。

6. 瓦尔特·本雅明："机械复制时代的艺术作品"，《〈单向街〉与其他作品》，阿米特·乔杜里编，J. A. 安德伍德译，伦敦、纽约：企鹅出版集团，2008 年，第228—259 页；"技术可复制时代的艺术作品"，《〈技术可复制时代的艺术作品〉与其他有关媒介研究的作品》，迈克尔·W.詹宁斯、布里吉德·多尔蒂和托马斯·Y.列文编，马萨诸塞州，坎布里奇：贝尔纳普出版社/哈佛大学出版社，2008 年。

7. 麦克斯·霍克海默："传统与批判理论"（1937 年），《论著选》，伦敦、纽约：康特纽姆出版社，1982 年，第 188—244 页（第 244 页）。

8. 本雅明："机械复制时代的艺术作品"，第 234 页。

9. 约翰·伯格：《观看之道》，伦敦：企鹅出版集团，1977 年，第 34 页。

10. 伯格：《观看之道》，第 34 页。

11. 约翰·克拉克："文化研究：英国的遗产"，《新时代与宿敌：文化研究与美国研究论文选》，纽约：哈珀·柯林斯出版集团，1991 年；罗伯特·W.迈克切斯尼："文化研究怎么了？"，《美国文化研究》，凯瑟琳·A.沃伦和玛丽·道格拉斯·瓦弗鲁斯编，芝加哥：伊利诺伊大学出版社，2002 年，第 76—93 页；卡里·尼尔森："已然存在的文化研究",《英国研究／文化研究:制度化异议》,以赛亚·史密森和南希·鲁芙编,芝加哥:伊利诺伊大学出版社,1994 年,第 191—206 页。

12. 相关评论文章参见:珍妮特·沃尔芙:"回忆录与微观学:瓦尔特·本雅明、女性主义与文化分析",《瓦尔特·本雅明:文化理论的批判式介入(第三辑:挪用)》,彼得·奥斯本编,伦敦:劳特利奇出版社,2005 年,第 319—333 页。

13. 乔纳森·弗兰岑:《纠正》,伦敦:新闻界出版社,2001 年,第 106 页。

14. 特里·伊格尔顿:《瓦尔特·本雅明,或走向革命批评》,伦敦:维尔索出版社,1981 年,第 ii 页。

15. 莱斯利:"屈服投降时代的艺术作品",第 1 页。

11 当代印迹

要点 🔑

- 《机械复制时代的艺术作品》依然是学界研究 20 世纪艺术、文化、技术和政治的重要参考文献。

- 近年来，陆续有学者对当前的本雅明研究提出批评，认为其普遍存在缺陷，即忽视本雅明著作中更为激进的内容。

- 学界同样争论不休的是，那些入门读本将本雅明思想局限于去政治化的阐述，究竟具有何种伦理意义？

地位

如今，《机械复制时代的艺术作品》依然被学界视为先锋之作，反复被各类选集收录，成为大学课堂的教材，并不断被论文转载引用。这一方面是由于该论著已为当前探讨艺术、技术与政治的关系奠定了深厚的学理基础。另一方面则是因为本雅明同时代的艺术家和作家大多深受其思想启迪。因而，但凡探讨 20 世纪早期艺术、电影、摄影和文学的著作，几乎都会提及《机械复制时代的艺术作品》，为数可观。例如，帕梅拉·考伊编选的论文集《机械复制时代的弗吉尼亚·伍尔芙》（2000）就运用本雅明的观点，来探讨技术可复制性在英国作家弗吉尼亚·伍尔芙 * 生平和创作中的重要意义。[1]同样，劳拉·菲格尔的《1930 至 1945 年的文学、电影和政治：影像之间的文学》（2010）一书也采用本雅明的观点，考察二战前夕以及战时电影和文学的关系。[2]

除了上述这些历史维度的研究，本雅明这篇论著还在探讨数字技术的著作中被提及。[3] 例如，罗夫·戈贝尔指出，本雅明认为新兴技术具有挑战现状的革命潜力，而如今"风靡世界的虚拟现实技术"恰能印证他的这一观点。在虚拟现实中，"原真性和独特性的'灵晕'——无论是艺术作品，抑或地理风貌——似乎都在逐渐消失。"[4]

这些新兴媒介能够发挥"增益"作用和"祛魅"（祛除由遥远之地带来的令人畏惧或摄人魂魄的陌生感）功效——使我们更容易和那些与众不同之物产生共鸣，从而纠正威权主义*统治者的国家对抗行为。[5] 与此同时，数字媒体还使政治骚乱或示威等特殊影像具有世界性意义，成为亲民主运动的象征而席卷全球。[6] "本雅明当年将"灵晕"的政治意义与法西斯主义联系在一起，这种通过大众媒介实现政治美学化的手段，如今成为民主主义自我言说的方式和反威权主义运动的路径。"[7]

> "'本雅明产业'的存在不足为奇。知识分子商品化是资本主义社会的普遍现象，尤其是在媒体大众化和教育普及化的时代，我们不仅能看见詹姆斯·乔伊斯冰箱贴玩偶，还能穿上西格蒙德·弗洛伊德拖鞋。"
>
> ——乌迪·E.格林伯格：《瓦尔特·本雅明产业的政治》

互动

当前，本雅明研究学者争议不断的焦点问题之一是，能否将其思想付诸研究一切反抗主流社会思潮的史实，并将所有文化现象置于其特定历史语境下展开考察。第二个问题是，当大学教育愈渐饱受压制，批判性思考频遭阻碍之际，本雅明研究是否仍具可能性。第三个问题则关乎是否有必要以批判性视角回顾本雅明研究**自身**的发展史，审视其是否亦遭受资本主义意识形态影响——其中存在不少悖论，即某些强烈反对资本主义消费文化的观点，反而被资本化（用以牟利）。

在 1997 年举行的国际瓦尔特·本雅明协会首届代表大会主旨发言中，本雅明研究专家苏珊·巴克-莫斯说，举办本雅明研究学术会议，在她看来颇具"讽刺"意味，因为本雅明本身是被学界边缘化的作家。[8] 她进一步指出，具有意义的本雅明研究必须立足于本雅明的这一观点，即"我们的做与不做，创造现实；我们的知与不知，形塑历史。两者有着千丝万缕的关联，因为我们如何构筑过去，将决定我们如何理解当下。"莫斯所谓的"我们"是指本雅明研究学者群体本身，她认为，学者们对《机械复制时代的艺术作品》的某些内容有所忽视，譬如文中对苏联社会主义艺术的探讨。

无独有偶，伊斯特·莱斯利在其诸多有关本雅明的论著中，也强调审视本雅明研究自身发展史的必要性。她还不断呼吁学界重视本雅明的革命政治论。最近，英国《卫报》记者斯图尔特·杰弗里斯就在其著作《深渊大酒店：法兰克福学派众生相》（2016）中，追溯了社会研究所的发展历程，并在全球政治普遍转型的时代背景下，考察法兰克福学派的理论观点在接受和运用过程中发生的变化。[9]

持续争议

究竟应该如何运用本雅明的思想观点，从根本上来说是一个伦理*问题。广义而言，所谓伦理，即指导个人行为的道德准则，乃基于我们自身的是非观念。有鉴于此，仍存在这样一个问题：当我们身处的环境（大学课堂、出版产业、学术会议）弥漫着资本主义商业氛围之时——这正是本雅明竭力反抗的对象，我们是否还有可能卓有成效地运用他的思想观点，并同时秉持他所捍卫的精神。例如，本雅明似乎已经无处不在，美术馆书店出售他的著作，新闻聚合网站 Buzzfeed* 发布他的"梗图"，这究竟是件好事——有助于进一步传播他的思想——还是标志着他的观点已遭混用？[10]

　　学者乌迪·E.格林伯格在其 2008 年撰写的论文《瓦尔特·本雅明产业的政治》中，对上述问题展开了探讨。他在考察学界对本雅明思想模糊不清的认识之前，首先分析其观点融入流行文化的过程（从实验音乐家、艺术家劳里·安德森 1987 年电影短片《我们究竟指谁》，到 2005 年流行歌剧《影子时代》对本雅明形象的最新刻画）。[11] 在格林伯格看来："过去 20 年间（1988 至 2008 年），这位德国犹太裔思想家已经脱离其政治背景，变成个体和意识形态认同的源泉，继而以社会化的面貌回归公众视野。"[12] 格林伯格还进一步分析出版物对本雅明理想形象的塑造，例如漫画《本雅明：初学者入门》（2001）和美国作家杰·帕里尼*的小说《本雅明的穿越》（1996）。在这些作品中，"这位激进思想家的生平和创作都以保守的形式来叙述，使本雅明不再是政治革命的符号，而成为社会疏离和迷失的象征。"[13]

1. 帕梅拉·考伊：《机械复制时代的弗吉尼亚·伍尔芙》，伦敦：劳特利奇出版社，2000 年。

2. 劳拉·菲格尔：《1930 至 1945 年的文学、电影和政治：影像之间的文学》，爱丁堡大学出版社，2010 年。

3. 弗雷亚·史威和亚历山德罗·福纳扎里编：《数字媒体、文化生产与投机资本主义》，伦敦：劳特利奇出版社，2013 年；姜在镐：《本雅明与媒介：现代性的奇观》，剑桥：政体出版社，2014 年；劳拉·J. 舍费尔德和凯特琳·汉密尔顿编：《理解数字化时代的大众文化与世界政治》，伦敦：劳特利奇出版社，2016 年。

4. 罗尔夫·戈贝尔："简介：本雅明其人"，《瓦尔特·本雅明论著指南》，罗尔夫·戈贝尔编，伦敦：卡姆登书屋，2009 年，第 1—22 页。

5. 戈贝尔：第 11 页。

6. 戈贝尔：第 11 页。

7. 戈贝尔：第 11 页。

8. 苏珊·巴克－莫斯："反斯大林主义的艺术：本雅明、肖斯塔科维奇，以及故事的结尾"，国际瓦尔特·本雅明协会第一次全体大会主旨演讲，阿姆斯特丹，1997 年 7 月。正式文稿题为"革命时代：前卫艺术与先锋派"，《本雅明研究》，第 1 辑，海尔格·盖耶－赖恩编，阿姆斯特丹：罗тел"匹出版社，2002 年，登录日期 2017 年 7 月 13 日，http://susanbuckmorss.info/text/antistalinist-art/。

9. 斯图尔特·杰弗里斯：《深渊大酒店：法兰克福学派众生相》，伦敦：维尔索出版社，2016 年。

10. 马特·奥蒂勒："瓦尔特·本雅明十一条发人深省的至理名言：今天纪念他的一百二十二周年诞辰，来获得一些'启迪'吧！"Buzzfeed，2014 年 7 月 15 日，登录日期 2017 年 6 月 30 日，https://www.buzzfeed. com/mattortile/work-of-art-in-the-age-of-social-discovery?utm_term=.vb8mqkAAj#.shK5pgyyD。

11. 乌迪·E. 格林伯格："瓦尔特·本雅明产业的政治"，《理论、文化与社会》第 25 卷，2008 年第 3 期：第 53—68 页，登录日期 2017 年 6 月 28 日，http://journals.sagepub.com.libproxy.ucl.ac.uk/doi/pdf/10.1177/0263276408090657，DOI: 10.1177/0263276408090657。

12. 格林伯格：第 61 页。

13. 格林伯格：第 68 页。

12 未来展望

要点 ⚘—

- 正如《机械复制时代的艺术作品》发表以来的历程一样，这篇论著未来在学界的接受也将不可避免地受到政治形势的影响。
- 新自由主义对怀疑主义的推崇，以及欧洲和美国极端右翼势力的兴起，都将成为本雅明研究进一步发展的契机。
- 对于想深入理解艺术、技术和政治之间的关系的人来说，《机械复制时代的艺术作品》是一部至关重要的参考文献。

潜力

在人文研究和社会科学领域，本雅明这篇论著的影响力经久不衰，充分体现其原创价值和观点的敏锐性，有助于我们理解该文发表以来，全球——至少是西方——政治经历的巨大转型。不仅如此，整个政治局势的演变，形塑着该文创作至今近一个世纪的接受过程，也将同样影响本雅明研究的未来发展方向。由是观之，20世纪80年代至90年代，新自由主义政治进入发展高潮时期，英语国家学界对于本雅明的解读趋于保守；如今，有迹象表明，这一趋势有所变化，更多激进视角的分析已经涌现。一方面是因为，2007至2008年全球金融危机*爆发以后，传媒界和学术界对自由市场观念（也即新自由主义）的批判，与当年本雅明对资本主义的批判不谋而合，甚至还直接借鉴了他的不少观点。[1] 另一方面则是由于，本雅明对法西斯主义操纵公共舆论的分析，恰有助于我们理解欧洲和美国正在兴起的极端右翼思潮——这一趋向往往与20世纪30年代的形势相提并论。[2]

最后值得一提的是，2015 年以来，本雅明的论著逐渐在学界之外引起广泛关注，此时正值唐纳德·特朗普首次宣布竞选美国总统。在大选期间和结果公布之后，众多评论文章都引述本雅明、阿多诺和霍克海默的观点，来诠释特朗普的诸种戏剧化表现，认为其与希特勒利用媒体充当宣传工具有颇多相似之处。[3]

一系列时事热点——全球金融危机和随之而来的财政紧缩*政策，导致欧洲大部分地区和美国的社会不公平现象日益加剧；极右势力以及希腊和西班牙极左势力相继崛起；还有美国大选——都使公众对本雅明思想的兴趣达到前所未有的热度。

> "大规模复制尤其得益于对大众的复制。如今，在大型游行和集会中，在体育赛事和战争中，大众的身影都被镜头捕捉下来，大众通过画面与自身相对而视。这一过程……与复制和摄影技术的发展密切相关。"
>
> ——瓦尔特·本雅明:《机械复制时代的艺术作品》

未来方向

如前文所述，有鉴于政治转型的时代背景，本雅明在后记中对战争和美学的探讨，可谓恰到好处，发人深省。本雅明在文中阐释道，"法西斯主义试图动员新生的无产阶级大众，而不去触及他们要求消灭的所有制关系。"[4]

为了实现这一目标，法西斯主义将领袖塑造成偶像，使暴力和一切具有"仪式价值"（此指一切与独裁政权有关的价值）的产物合法化。于是，不仅传统的艺术形式被用于意识形态宣传，连电影和其他大众媒介亦是如此。本雅明由是指出，惟有战争"能在保持所有制关系不变的前提下，充分动员当前的所有技术资源。"[5] 艺术和技术有助于维持看似不可更迭的政治地位，使绝大多数民众向少数既得利益者俯首称臣。

若将本雅明有关艺术、技术和战争的观点深入付诸 21 世纪的政治研究，依然存在诸多书写空间。不过，学者和新闻记者已进一步拓展研究疆域，着手探究特朗普如何通过营造"景观"来获取并操控权力。[6] 例如，乔尔·彭尼在新著《公民营销者：社交媒体时代的政治舆论宣传》（2017）中运用本雅明的政治美学化理论，来分析特朗普的宣传技巧，包括雇人参加他宣布竞选的那场集会等。[7] 马克·安德烈赫维奇 * 则采用本雅明的观点来探讨特朗普的媒体形象，及其竞选中具有煽动 * 意味的内容。[8] 同样，人类学家唐娜·M. 戈尔茨坦和柯拉·霍尔亦使用本雅明这篇论著，以及本雅明研究专家苏珊·巴克-莫斯的观点，来考察特朗普的"治国奇观"。[9]

除此之外，本雅明在文中提及革命性力量的观点，似乎也已被用来研究手机和其他视听录音设备，审视其如何捕捉和分享我们的日常生活动态。其实在这篇论著中，本雅明早就提过相似看法。他探讨"编辑信箱"和其他读者互动形式在 19 世纪末和 20 世纪初的盛行，并指出"越来越多的读者变成作者"。[10]

事实上，早在互联网诞生 60 年前，本雅明在一篇文章中描述过类似画面，至少与一部分当代网络博客作者的生活场景不谋而合。他如是写道："但凡是有工作有收入的欧洲人，现在原则上都有机会在某个地方发表工作心得，抒发胸中苦闷，撰写新闻报道等诸如此类的作品。"[11]

小结

出乎意料的是，自《机械复制时代的艺术作品》发表以来的数十年间，本雅明的革命乐观主义思想并没有促成颠覆性的变革。电影则超越本雅明的期待，变成一种更为反动的媒介。多年以来，学者们在研究这篇论著时采用的术语，恰是本雅明所竭力反对的概念。他们更关注本雅明对艺术接受模式变化的论述，而忽视随之而来的政治后果。由是观之，尽管本雅明抱有良好的写作初衷，但这篇论著已被学界所混用，并非旨在反对法西斯主义，其目标实则更趋保守——换言之，这些批评家根本无意改变现状。

尽管《机械复制时代的艺术作品》的接受过程存在些许遗憾，但它依然是艺术史和文学研究领域的扛鼎之作，也是衡量当今艺术批评是否真正具有批判性的试金石。不仅如此，这篇论著还为文化研究、媒介研究和政治美学等领域奠定了基础，催生出一系列崭新的研究视角来看待电视、名人文化、"用户生成内容"*和"模因"*等各类现象。本雅明所提出的概念术语，诸如灵晕消逝、偶像价值和仪式价值等，依然为艺术史学者所采用。而他在广播、电影和摄影兴起的年代对政治美学化所做的定义，亦成为电视、社交媒体和真人秀盛行的当代，我们探究政治的学理依据。有鉴于此，《机械复制时代的艺术作品》这篇论著依然能给我们带来诸多启迪，不仅对我们认识艺术、理解新兴媒介大有裨益，还有助于探讨艺术和新兴媒介如何改变我们的世界观——究竟是更加积极进取，还是愈发消极遁世？

1. 罗杰·伯科维茨和汤·N.托艾编：《全球金融危机的思想根源》，纽约：福特汉姆大学出版社，2013 年，第 164—165 页；菲利普·米罗斯基：《永远不要浪费一场严重危机：新自由主义如何度过金融危机》，伦敦：维尔索出版社，2013 年，第 84 页，第 100 页；米丽亚姆·迈斯纳：《叙述全球金融危机：都市想象与神话政治》，纽约和贝辛斯托克：帕尔格雷夫出版公司，2017 年，第 21 页，第 40—45 页。

2. 相关评论文章参见：约翰·帕尔默："欧洲极端右翼政党崛起是 20 世纪 30 年代令人不寒而栗的回声"，《卫报》，2013 年 11 月 15 日，登录日期 2017 年 6 月 30 日，https://www.theguardian.com/commentisfree/2013/nov/15/far-right-threat-europe-integration；彼得·福斯特："欧洲极端右翼势力崛起绝非虚惊一场"，《每日电讯报》，2016 年 5 月 19 日，登录日期 2017 年 6 月 30 日，http://www.telegraph.co.uk/news/2016/05/19/the-rise-of-the-far-right-in-europe-is-not-a-false-alarm/；马克·马德尔："法西斯主义、20 世纪 30 年代和 21 世纪"，《BBC 新闻》，2016 年 12 月 20 日，登录日期 2017 年 6 月 30 日，http://www.bbc.co.uk/news/uk-politics-38317787；"不，这不是 19 世纪 30 年代，但确实是法西斯主义"，牛津大学历史系，2016 年 11 月 16 日，登录日期 2017 年 6 月 30 日，http://www.history.ox.ac.uk/article/no-isnt-1930s-yes-fascism。

3. 亚历山大·宾内特："唐纳德·特朗普与法西斯主义美学：这位 20 世纪马克思主义艺术评论家教我们如何看懂那位 21 世纪总统候选人"，《在这些时代》，2016 年 1 月 28 日，登录日期 2017 年 6 月 28 日，http://inthesetimes.com/article/18807/donald-trump-and-the-aesthetics-of-fascism；托马斯·杜姆："堕落的法西斯主义、虚无主义与唐纳德·特朗普"，《当代境遇》，2015 年 9 月，登录日期 2017 年 6 月 28 日，http://contemporarycondition.blogspot.co.uk/2015/09/degraded-fascism-nihilism-and-donald.html；亚历克斯·罗斯："法兰克福学派预知特朗普的出现"，《纽约客》，2016 年 12 月 5 日，登录日期 2017 年 6 月 28 日，http://www.newyorker.com/culture/cultural-comment/the-frankfurt-school-knew-trump-was-coming。

4. 瓦尔特·本雅明："机械复制时代的艺术作品"，《启迪》，汉娜·阿伦特编，伦敦：皮姆里科出版社，1999 年，第 234 页。

5. 本雅明："机械复制时代的艺术作品"，第 234 页。

6. 案例参见：大卫·丹比："反对美国的阴谋：特朗普的修辞术"，《纽约客》，2015 年 12 月 15 日，登录日期 2017 年 6 月 30 日，http://www.newyorker.com/

culture/cultural-comment/plot-america-donald-trumps-rhetoric；奥利弗·琼斯：《唐纳德·特朗普：修辞术》，伦敦：眼镜出版社，2016年；罗纳德·布朗斯坦："特朗普有关白人怀旧主义的说辞"，《大西洋月刊》，2016年6月2日，登录日期2017年6月30日，https://www.theatlantic.com/politics/archive/2016/06/trumps-rhetoric-of-white-nostalgia/485192/；山姆·利斯："特朗普的修辞术：无意识的胜利"，《卫报》，2017年1月13日，登录日期2017年6月30日，https://www.theguardian.com/us-news/2017/jan/13/donald-trumps-rhetoric-how-being-inarticulate-is-seen-as-authentic。

7. 乔尔·彭尼：《公民营销者：社交媒体时代的政治舆论宣传》，牛津：牛津大学出版社，2017年，第113页。

8. 马克·安德烈赫维奇："特朗普的快感"，《电视与新媒体》第17卷，2016年第7期：第651—655页。

9. 唐娜·M. 戈尔茨坦和柯拉·霍尔："选举后的超现实主义和唐纳德·特朗普掌控的怀旧种族主义"，《HAU：民族志理论》第7卷，2017年第1期：http://dx.doi.org/10.14318/hau7.1.026。

10. 本雅明："机械复制时代的艺术作品"，第225页。

11. 本雅明："机械复制时代的艺术作品"，第225页。

术语表

1. **政治美学化**：本雅明提出的术语（贝托尔特·布莱希特曾给予帮助），指法西斯领袖使用煽动性的宣传攻势，迫使民众效忠国家，并使其忽视自身遭受的压迫政策。这一概念是本雅明在《机械复制时代的艺术作品》中的核心论点。

2. **反犹太主义**：对犹太人抱有偏见、敌意和歧视，包括秉持根深蒂固的刻板印象（如"犹太人都是吝啬鬼"），使用带有偏见性的表达（如"to Jew someone down"表示讨价还价），乃至采取暴力行为、实施歧视性法律等。

3. **《拱廊街计划》**（1927—）：本雅明未完成的遗作。他认为巴黎商业拱廊街是19世纪资本主义现代性的象征，并计划对其详加考察。

4. **艺术批评**：对艺术作品的批评，形式包括学术论著和公共评论（如报刊文章）。本雅明这篇论著即是艺术批评文章，也是对传统艺术批评的批评。

5. **"为艺术而艺术"**：19世纪法国兴起的艺术观念，认为艺术作品具有永恒不变的内在价值，独立于任何道德功用或功利目的。本雅明这篇论著对这一观念提出批评，认为它容易被混用，为法西斯主义服务。

6. **艺术史**：研究视觉艺术发展史的学科，包括绘画和雕塑。本雅明这篇论著试图重新勾勒艺术史的面貌，将艺术生产的物质环境纳入研究视野。

7. **灵晕**：本雅明在《机械复制时代的艺术作品》中提出的概念，其含义难以捉摸。它意指艺术作品的原创性、来源并高于生活的独特性，以及迫使观众产生敬畏感的权威性。灵晕与艺术作品的膜拜价值和仪式作用相关——历史上艺术作品是宗教仪轨、皇室礼仪或其他古老仪式的重要组成部分。（也译作"光韵""灵光"等——译者注）

8. **紧缩**：经济学术语，指政府缩减公共服务开支（例如，社会福利、公共住房和医疗服务等）。

9. **《作为生产者的作家》**：瓦尔特·本雅明的论著。文中提出的观点在后来的《机械复制时代的艺术作品》中得到进一步拓展。他特别强调，不存在完全自律或毫无政治倾向的艺术。相较于《机械复制时代的艺术作品》和他的其他作品，这篇论著以更为正统的方式表达其马克思主义立场。

10. **威权主义**：一种政体形式，要求民众绝对服从其权威，限制个人自由。法西斯主义是一种具有暴力色彩和民族主义倾向的威权主义。在本雅明这篇论著的第一稿中，所有指称"法西斯主义"的表达均被替换为"威权主义"。

11. **自律／自律性**：独立／独立性；本雅明使用该术语特指艺术独立于／脱离日常生活的唯美主义观点，即"为艺术而艺术"的立场。

12. **先锋派**（参见"欧洲先锋派"）

13. **Buzzfeed**：总部位于纽约的美国网络新闻媒体公司，专门从事社会新闻和娱乐，尤其关注数字媒体和技术。（暂无官方译名，有媒体译作"嗡嗡喂"——译者注）

14. **资本主义**：一种经济体制，产业和贸易活动由拥有产品和服务的私人和团体所决定，而非由国家控制。贸易活动开展的场所被称为市场。

15. **资本主义生产方式**：以生产资料私有制（非国有制）为特征的生产方式，即生产资料拥有者（资产阶级）通过抽取劳动者（无产阶级）创造／出售的剩余价值（利润率）来积累财富。

16. **《夏尔·波德莱尔：巴黎风光》**（1923）：瓦尔特·本雅明曾以德语翻译法国诗人夏尔·波德莱尔（1821—1867）的诗集《巴黎风光》。波德莱尔对本雅明具有重要影响，多次出现在其论著中，包括他未完成的遗作《拱廊街计划》（1927— ）。

17. **冷战**（1947—1991）：第二次世界大战之后，西方阵营（美国及其北约盟国）和东方阵营（苏联、东德和中国）之间爆发的激烈军事冲突和政治对抗。随着 1991 年苏联解体，冷战正式结束。

18. **殖民主义**：一个国家对另一个国家实施统治的手段，包括统治者（殖民者）和被统治者（殖民地）之间的不平等关系，以及通过开采殖民地的各种资源来强化宗主国的经济等。

19. **拼贴画**：将不同物质媒介上不相关的片段（报章、杂志、剪贴等）粘合而创作的视觉艺术作品。拼贴画作为一种艺术形式兴起于 20 世纪早期。最初的实践者试图通过混淆艺术和日常生活的界限，来挑战资本主义。

20. **商品化**：将事物转换成商品（可买卖流通或谋取利益）的过程。本雅明在其著作中探讨如何剥离商品的谋利属性，并用以抵制资本主义。

21. **商品拜物教**：资本主义社会中社会关系转变为利益交换的现象。根据马克思的说法，资本主义将人与人之间的社会关系，转变为物与物之间的经济关系。而本雅明所感兴趣的是，事物如何能够脱离其谋利本质，而实现革命目的。

22. **共产主义**：最初由卡尔·马克思提出的经济制度，生产资料（如自然资源、工厂、机械设备等）归集体所有。在马克思的设想中，共产主义社会不存在阶级之分。本雅明这篇论著基于共产主义理想而提出一种艺术理论，来对抗法西斯主义的政治美学化理念。

23. **《无处不在的征服》**（1928）：法国作家保罗·瓦雷里（1871—1945）的论作，其内容主要探讨技术对日常生活的影响。同时，他还对未来的技术发展作出预测。本雅明在文中引述了瓦雷里的观点。

24. **征用**：将小型（通常指弱势）团体和个人的观点或作品进行挪用或同化的手段。本雅明这篇论著旨在创立一种艺术理论，使之不不会被用来为法西斯主义服务。

25. **批判理论**：本雅明和法兰克福学派同仁于 20 世纪 30 年代共同创立的学科，旨在超越以解释现象为特征的"传统理论"，积极寻求纠正社会弊病的方法，如阶级不平等、权力滥用等。

26. **文化研究**：运用跨学科方法（借鉴社会科学和人文研究范式）来研究当代（尤其是大众）文化的学术领域（《牛津英语词典》）。

27. **《文化工业》**：麦克斯·霍克海默和西奥多·阿多诺合著的论作。文中指出，在资本主义制度下，大众文化成为一种工业，旨在使大众获得安抚，并接受现状。

28. **达达主义**：20世纪早期的文学艺术运动，通过颠覆传统的创作方式，使公众感到惊吓、震颤乃至愤怒。这场运动一方面是回应第一次世界大战引发的社会恐慌，另一方面则是挑战艺术商品化和资本主义对日常生活的侵蚀——这一切都对瓦尔特·本雅明影响颇深。

29. **煽动**：一种利用公众的情绪、偏见和本能，而非通过逻辑来宣传游说的操纵手段，多与政治独裁者和伪善政客等人物相关联。

30. **去政治／去政治化**：撇开政治因素来看待某个活动或文化现象。例如，对一段文本展开去政治化分析，忽略其政治层面，包括文中任何政治性表述，而关注其他内容。

31. **分神消遣**：使人对目标事物无法专心；注意力无法集中的状态。法兰克福学派对资本主义制度下大众文化具有的分神消遣作用颇感兴趣；本雅明认为分神消遣有可能具有积极意义。

32. **伦理／伦理学**：指导我们行为的道德准则（旨在明辨是非）；研究道德准则如何建立或贯彻的学问。

33. **欧洲先锋派**：泛指1910年至第二次世界大战期间，欧洲具有激进倾向或逆主流文化的艺术和文学思潮，包括立体主义、达达主义、超现实主义和未来主义运动。这些运动都具有共同的特征，即以颠覆传统的形式开展艺术创作。（也译作"前卫派"——译者注）

34. **法西斯主义**：右翼威权政体。瓦尔特·本雅明生前对法西斯主义在欧洲的兴起和发展尤为担忧，并对法西斯主义使用意识形态宣传、军事力量美学化（"美化"军事力量）和怀旧意象（诱使大众留恋过去）等手段极为关注。

35. **漫游者**：直译自法语"flâneur"。该术语首次由夏尔·波德莱尔所用，以定义在城市中步行的现代性体验。本雅明借用其概念来理解19世纪的城市。他认为，随着巴黎商业拱廊街被弃置，加之法定工作时间制度的普遍采用，导致真正的"漫游者"消失不在。

36. **法兰克福学派**：指多位重要的左翼哲学家和理论家——这些著作等身、影响深远的学者最初于20世纪20年代至30年代聚集在美茵河畔法兰克福大学，诸如德国哲学家麦克斯·霍克海默（1895—1973）和西奥多·阿多诺（1903—1969），他们均是瓦尔特·本雅明的同仁。

37. **未来主义**：20世纪早期兴起于意大利的实验艺术运动，崇尚速度、技术和战争。该运动的发起者认为意大利应成为欧洲具有领导地位的政治力量。这一思潮的兴起与贝尼托·墨索里尼的法西斯政党息息相关。

38. **类型**：源自法语，意为"种类"，指艺术作品的分类，例如"悬疑""喜剧""悲剧""浪漫""西部"等。评论家通常考察同一类型中的不同艺术作品，继而判断其是否遵从或挑战所属艺术类型的惯常模式。

39. **盖世太保**：纳粹统治时期德国和欧洲占领地区的秘密国家警察组织（"Geheime Staatspolizei"的缩写，德语意为"秘密国家警察"）。盖世太保设立于1933年，并于1945年5月随德国战败而解散。

40. **全球金融危机**（2007—2008）：爆发于美国并席卷欧洲大部分地区的金融危机。有专家认为这是20世纪30年代大萧条以来最为严重的一场经济动荡，其导火索是由于监管宽松致使次级房屋借贷市场（向不具备还款能力的借款人提供贷款）和银行业同时出现危机。这场危机使资本主义自由市场制度再次受到批评。

41. **大萧条**：20世纪30年代在美国和欧洲持续蔓延的一场经济衰退，起始于1929年股市崩盘，直至第二次世界大战后才正式得以复苏。大萧条期间，正是由于民不聊生，法西斯得以成功推行民族主义和排外主义政策，使民众相信少数族裔和犹太人是造成更大系统性风险的罪魁祸首。

42. **高雅文化**：精英阶层创作或享有的艺术作品，被视为独特而稀有，比大众文化更具优越感，后者所涉对象为广大普通民众。

43. **历史主义**：宽泛而言，历史主义认为一切社会事件和现象的发生均是历史发展使然。本雅明对这一观点持批评态度，他认为若要充分理解过去发生的事件，就必须考虑促使这些事件产生的物质（社会经济）背景。

44. **社会研究所**：该机构是 20 世纪上半叶德国知识分子的聚集之地，位于美茵河畔法兰克福大学。自 1930 年以来，在麦克斯·霍克海默（1895—1973）的领导下，社会研究所将马克思主义哲学和弗洛伊德精神分析学相结合开展研究。该机构的一众学者被称为"法兰克福学派"。

45. **犹太神秘主义**：研究犹太民族历史上不同形式神秘主义现象的学科。学者们普遍认为，该学科的创建者是本雅明的挚友兼同事哥舒姆·舒勒姆（1897—1982），起点是他的著作《犹太神秘主义主流》（1941）。

46. **《罗马晚期的工艺美术》**（1905）：艺术史学家阿洛伊斯·李格尔（1858—1905）的著作，主要通过大型纪念碑和皮带扣等日常物品，来探讨如何理解古罗马晚期的艺术。他的研究方法基于一种假设，即并非价值高昂的物品才值得被研究。这一观点使瓦尔特·本雅明颇受启发。

47. **文学研究**：对文学作品展开研究、阐释和评价，包括文本形式特征分析、反思和质疑文化成规，和／或探究其社会政治和历史影响。

48. **马克思主义**（参见"西方马克思主义"）

49. **马克思主义文学批评**：将马克思主义思想付诸文学文本分析，通常重视文本内有关社会经济关系的描述，从中反映文本生产的物质经济环境。

50. **大众文化**：以共有／集体方式接受同一媒介（包括新闻源、艺术、音乐或文学）而产生的价值观和思想。"大众"一词意味着这种文化由广大普通民众自发生成，而非自上而下强加而成——本雅明在这篇论著中对此观点展开探讨。

51. 模因：广义而言，即在某种文化中迅速传播的思想、观念或表达。常用以指称（通常是恶搞式）网络图片、视频和文本，它们通过互联网复制、修改和传播。（也译"弥母""迷因""觅母"等——译者注）。

52. 蒙太奇：类似拼贴画*的文学和电影技法，完全由片段、图像、文本或其他媒体形式所构成。对电影而言，包括剪接、修改或图像编辑等形式。对文学而言，主要指将互不关联的文本拼接在一起。

53. 民族主义：主张本民族优越于其他民族，对民族的效忠高于一切；是爱国主义的极端形式。本雅明生前正值法西斯主义运动高涨之际，其核心思想即是民族主义。

54. 国家社会主义德国工人党：也称"纳粹党"；德国极端右翼政党，活跃于 1920 至 1945 年间，20 世纪 30 年代在阿道夫·希特勒的领导下成为执政党。该党的创立旨在吸引工人阶层脱离共产党，最初以反资本主义、反资产阶级（中产阶级）和民族主义为宗旨。但随着希特勒上台，该党的主导思想转向反犹太主义和反马克思主义。

55. 新自由主义：也称"自由市场资本主义"，是资本主义的一种表现形式，其特征是国家干预较小。新自由主义者认为，市场具有自我调节功能，参与市场的个人或企业无需受到过多规则或监管限制。

56. 《纽约客》：创刊于 1925 年的美国综合杂志，内容涵盖散文、讽刺作品、小说、评论、漫画和诗歌等，出版方现为康泰纳仕集团。《纽约客》在思想文化领域颇具影响力：1968 年，汉娜·阿伦特在该杂志上发表有关瓦尔特·本雅明的文章，使之成为知识界家喻户晓的人物。

57. 《现代生活的画家》（1863）：法国诗人夏尔·波德莱尔的名作。书中，波德莱尔呼吁艺术家改变创作技法，以便更充分地传达现代城市生活体验。本雅明著作中有关 19 世纪巴黎的内容，就引自这部作品。

58. **巴黎商业拱廊街**：19 世纪初巴黎市中心兴建的一系列装有玻璃拱顶的街道，旨在迎合新中产阶级的购物需求。随着 19 世纪后半叶百货公司的出现，这些拱廊街被悉数空置。

59. **1968 年 5 月巴黎起义**：史称"五月风暴"。最初是巴黎高中和大学爆发的一系列学生抗议事件，其后愈演愈烈，演变为长达数月的学生示威活动，旨在抨击法国教育体制中精英主义泛滥的现状。

60. **政治美学**：研究艺术和政治之间的关系——政治思想如何在艺术中表现？政治运动如何采用艺术化手段，或招募艺术家，来宣扬特定的意识形态？《机械复制时代的艺术作品》即是一部有关政治美学的论作，本雅明随之成为该领域的思想先驱。

61. **精神分析学**：通过分析有意识的行为和无意识的思想、冲动或欲望之间的关系，来治疗精神紊乱等病症的思想体系。在本雅明那个时代，精神分析学对诸多艺术文学思潮产生了重要影响，尤其是超现实主义。本雅明自己也将精神分析学的观点融入写作中，来探讨现代艺术、文学和 19 世纪的巴黎。

62. **激进**：脱离传统；割裂过去；寻求改变现状；从根本上改变某些东西。本雅明在著作中秉持激进主张，致力于探究可复制性如何能被用以反抗法西斯主义，彻底改变社会现状。

63. **反动**：右翼、保守，以及其他反对社会改革或进步的主张。本雅明通过其论著试图抗击法西斯主义宣扬历史虚构的反动倾向，主张利用电影和摄影来积极推动社会变革。

64. **国会大厦**：德国柏林的历史建筑，建成于 1894 年，原为德意志帝国的帝国议会会址。1933 年，纳粹党纵火将其焚毁。

65. **修辞术**：有说服力的演讲或写作艺术，包括利用修辞手段和特定意象来唤起公众共鸣。20 世纪 30 年代后期，法西斯主义者采用各种宣传攻势来主导公共舆论。本雅明对此颇感兴趣，他认为这种手段借鉴了传统艺术批评中的诸多观点。修辞术也被本雅明视为现代史上政治美学化的表征。

66. **社会主义**：以生产资料公有制、分配交易集体化为特征的经济模式。

根据马克思主义理论，社会主义是推翻资本主义、实现共产主义之间的过渡阶段。

67. **苏联**：一党执政的马克思列宁主义国家，由东欧地区的 15 个社会主义加盟共和国组成，自 1922 年成立，至 1991 年解体。

68. **定格**：戏剧家贝托尔特·布莱希特提出的术语，指戏剧表演过程中将情节暂停的这段特殊时刻，旨在震醒观众，使之意识到这是演出，也给予观众时间，对舞台上发生的一切进行评判。本雅明对这一概念有过充分论述，并促使他思考机械复制时代的观看行为。（也译作"停顿""凝滞"等——译者注）

69. **超现实主义**：20 世纪早期兴起于巴黎的艺术运动，以逆主流文化为特征，作为对消费文化和艺术商品化的回应。这场运动试图挑战现实和非现实、外部世界和无意识思想、乃至生活与艺术之间的界限。这些观点深受浪漫主义的思潮影响。

70. **技巧**：在艺术领域，指艺术作品（绘画、小说、雕塑等）的创作手法，诸如使用粗线条绘图、使用长句写作、或保持雕塑的粗糙边缘等。其概念与"内容"恰好相反，后者指艺术作品真正想要传达的内涵。

71. **机械复制**：通过技术手段（比如摄影术）来复制艺术作品，而非手工复制（例如，通过重新绘制另一幅图像来复制画作）。

72. **《历史哲学论纲》**（1940）：本雅明的代表作，主要内容是批判历史主义，并驳斥将历史视为"一系列连锁事件"的线性演进观。

73. **命题**：论文、演讲或其他书面／口语作品试图表达的主张。在本雅明的论著中，命题是其"辩证法"的一部分，即通过分析两种全然相反的观点来寻求真相。

74. **极权主义**：一种政权集中化的制度，迫使公民完全臣服于国家。威权主义指个人或小型团体垄断政权，而极权主义则指个人／团体寻求对全部社会生活的掌控，并利用全部民众来实现其目的。

75. **《传统与批判理论》**（1937）：法兰克福学派领袖麦克斯·霍克海默的论作，文中抨击常见于自然科学的理论方法（包括观察法和解

释法等),认为其有悖于他所谓的"批判理论"。后者旨在挑战现状,尤其是资本主义制度。瓦尔特·本雅明的论著即遵循批判理论的方法。

76. **城市化**:指农村地区转变为城镇的过程,以及城镇发展与扩张所带来的转型作用。本雅明的许多论著都致力于考察资本主义制度下的城市生活体验,尤其关注巴黎如何成为 19 世纪欧洲资本主义的象征中心。

77. **用户生成内容**:指媒介内容均为媒介平台或出版载体的观众或"用户"创作,而非来自专业作家。该术语常用于指称网络媒体——尤其是社交媒体——同时也适用于早期的媒介形式,诸如 19 世纪初报纸和杂志刊登的"读者来信"等。

78. **越南战争**(1955—1975):1955 至 1975 年间,越南北部共产主义政权与南部资本主义政权在老挝、柬埔寨和越南等地爆发的战争,正值冷战时期*。自 20 世纪 60 年代中期起,欧洲和美国便发起反战示威,直至战争结束演变为更为广泛的反体制思潮,包括质疑传统和权威。正是在这一背景下,本雅明的《机械复制时代的艺术作品》首个英译本问世。

79. **《观看之道》**:英国广播公司 1972 年播出的电视系列片,由文化评论家约翰·伯格主持。1973 年,伯格将其改编成同名著作。这部电视系列片和同名著作都旨在批判传统艺术史,为此还大量引用了瓦尔特·本雅明的论作。

80. **西德**:也称"德意志联邦共和国",是现今德国的部分地区,冷战*时期与其他资本主义国家属于同一阵营。西德自 1949 年 5 月 23 日成立,于 1990 年 10 月 3 日柏林墙倒塌后与东德统一。柏林墙曾将西德与属于共产主义阵营的东德隔开,并将柏林这座城市一分为二,一部分隶属西德,另一部分隶属东德。

81. **西方马克思主义**:西欧与中欧地区兴起的哲学流派,这些学者运用马克思主义理论,但与苏联式的马克思主义哲学家有所区别。20 世纪 50 年代,法国哲学家莫里斯·梅洛-庞蒂提出这一术语,并追根溯源,用以定义本雅明和其他法兰克福学派学者的作品。

82. **第一次世界大战（1914—1918）**：协约国（以俄罗斯帝国、法国、意大利、美国和英国为首）和同盟国（以德国和奥匈帝国为首）之间爆发的全球性战争。德国战败后，经济遭受破坏，导致民众日趋贫困，这也成为法西斯主义崛起的诱因。

83. **第二次世界大战（1939—1945）**：同盟国（以苏联、英国和美国为首）与轴心国（以德国、意大利和日本为首）之间爆发的全球性战争，致使欧洲全境七百万犹太人惨遭屠杀。

人名表

1. **西奥多·阿多诺**（1903—1969），德国著名哲学家、社会学家和马克思主义评论家，因与麦克斯·霍克海默合著《启蒙辩证法：哲学断片》一书而最为称道。他是法兰克福社会研究所的领导者，亦是瓦尔特·本雅明的好友。

2. **汉娜·阿伦特**（1906—1975），美籍德裔犹太作家和政治理论家，以其关于纳粹、极权主义和暴力的研究而著称。她是《选集》（本雅明论著选，其中包括首次发表的《机械复制时代的艺术作品》）首个英译本的编辑。

3. **尤金·阿特盖**（1857—1927），法国纪实摄影先驱，以拍摄巴黎未被拆除、重新开发或进行现代化升级的街道和建筑而著称。本雅明援引其照片，作为现代艺术具有政治内涵的明证。

4. **乔治·巴代伊**（1897—1962），具有先锋色彩的法国作家和知识分子。希特勒掌权之际，他是巴黎中央图书馆的馆员。本雅明逃离巴黎时将手稿悉数托付给巴代伊。

5. **夏尔·波德莱尔**（1821—1867），法国散文家、诗人和艺术评论家，以描绘现代性和城市而广为人知。波德莱尔的作品对本雅明具有深刻影响。他曾写过多篇与波德莱尔有关的文章，并翻译其诗歌作品。

6. **约翰·伯格**（1926—2017），英国作家、艺术家、评论家和政治活动家。他在艺术批评领域著述颇丰，还写有不少小说、诗歌和纪实文学作品，其代表作是基于《机械复制时代的艺术作品》而创作的《观看之道》。

7. **贝托尔特·布莱希特**（1898—1956），德国马克思主义戏剧家、诗人和戏剧导演，亦是瓦尔特·本雅明的挚友。他因倡导戏剧叙事改革而著称，往往与欧洲先锋运动联系在一起。他还鲜明批判资本主义、中产阶级价值观和纳粹德国政权，同样为人所称道。

8. **苏珊·巴克−莫斯**，美国文化历史学家和哲学家，也是著名的瓦尔特·本雅明研究学者，著有《消极辩证法的起源:西奥多·阿多诺、瓦尔特·本雅明和法兰克福学派》(1977) 和《观看的辩证法：瓦尔特·本雅明和拱廊街计划》(1989)。她极力批判美国艺术和文学研究学者对本雅明作品的去政治化解读。

9. **乔治·布什**（1924—2018），美国共和党政治家，1989 至 1993 年为第 41 任美国总统。

10. **特里·伊格尔顿**（1943 年生），英国马克思主义文学批评家和兰卡斯特大学特聘教授，曾师从马克思主义文学批评家雷蒙德·威廉斯，以文学理论和马克思主义文学研究而著称。伊格尔顿于 1981 年出版有关本雅明的论著，强调其激进主义特征。

11. **霍华德·艾兰**，哈佛大学文学教授、瓦尔特·本雅明作品的主要译者和编辑，包括《拱廊街计划》首个英译本。艾兰还合著有一部本雅明传记，题为《瓦尔特·本雅明：批判的一生》。

12. **弗里德里希·恩格斯**（1820—1895），德国哲学家、卡尔·马克思（1818—1883）的亲密同事，因与其合著《共产党宣言》(1848) 而著称。恩格斯和马克思的论著对本雅明影响深刻。

13. **乔纳森·弗兰岑**（1959 年生），美国小说家，因其屡获奖项的作品《纠正》(2001) 而声名鹊起。小说中，主人公将所有批判理论的著作悉数出售，包括瓦尔特·本雅明的作品，旨在为高昂的约会提供开支。这被视为讽刺 20 世纪 90 年代批判理论在美国的没落现状，而这恰是一个异常繁荣的时代。

14. **埃里希·弗罗姆**（1900—1980），德国哲学家、心理学家和社会学家，法兰克福学派学者。他的第一部作品《逃避自由》(1941) 被视为首部政治心理学论著。他后来的作品《爱的艺术》亦使其广为人知。

15. **阿道夫·希特勒**（1889—1945），1934 至 1945 年任德国国家元首，因对七百万犹太人实施屠杀和种族灭绝而声名狼藉。由于纳粹政权剥夺所有犹太人的德国国籍，本雅明被迫于 1933 年 3 月逃亡海外。他在从法国逃往西班牙的途中自杀，死因成谜。

16. 麦克斯·霍克海默（1895—1973），德国著名犹太裔左翼社会学家和哲学家，亦是"法兰克福学派"的领导者。最为人熟知的作品是他与西奥多·阿多诺合著的《启蒙辩证法：哲学断片》（1947）。在与阿多诺的合作下，他还出版本雅明的首部论作集，并资助他的其他研究。

17. 齐格弗里德·克拉考尔（1889—1966），德国犹太裔文化评论家、社会学家、电影理论家和记者，代表作有论文集《大众装饰》（1963）。他是本雅明的好友，但并不赞同本雅明对大众文化的积极解读，认为大众文化的分神消遣特质实则有助于防止大众起身反抗。

18. 伊斯特·莱斯利（1964 年生），瓦尔特·本雅明研究的领军人物，伦敦大学伯贝克学院政治美学教授。莱斯利现已出版多部有关本雅明的著作，专注解读其作品的政治意涵，致力于使本雅明研究重归政治化的研究路径。

19. 格奥尔格·卢卡奇（1885—1971），匈牙利哲学家和文学批评家，其著名的《历史与阶级意识：马克思主义辩证法研究》是西方马克思主义传统的奠基之作，但他晚年否认其早期作品属于这一思潮。

20. 赫伯特·马尔库塞（1898—1979），美籍德裔犹太哲学家、马克思主义理论家，法兰克福学派代表人物。20 世纪 60 年代，他曾参与法国、德国和美国的学生运动。1933 年，他逃离纳粹德国，并于 1940 年获得美国国籍。

21. 卡尔·马克思（1818—1883），德国政治哲学家和经济学家。他对资本主义阶级关系的分析，及其对平均主义社会制度的阐述，为共产主义奠定了基础。他与弗里德里希·恩格斯（1820—1895）共同发表《共产党宣言》（1848）；并在《资本论》（1867—1894）中充分阐述其有关生产和阶级关系的理论。

22. 莫里斯·梅洛-庞蒂（1908—1961），法国现象学哲学家和作家，也是当时唯一将描述心理学付诸研究的学者。庞蒂深受马克思主义影响，被认为是"西方马克思主义"概念的提出者。

23. 杰·帕里尼（1948 年生），美国学者和作家，以文学批评、诗歌和传记小说而著称。1997 年，帕里尼出版有关瓦尔特·本雅明的传记小说，讲述其 1940 年逃离巴黎的历程，题为《本雅明的穿越》。

24. 朵拉·苏菲·波拉客（1890—1964），瓦尔特·本雅明的妻子，两人于 1918 年结婚，1928 年离婚。期间，由于收入不稳定，加之本雅明旅居海外写作，两人长期分离，致使婚姻关系破裂。两人育有一子，名叫斯特凡。

25. 阿洛伊斯·李格尔（1858—1905），奥地利艺术史学家和理论家，是艺术史作为独立学科而存在的关键人物，代表作有《风格问题》（1893）和《罗马晚期的工艺美术》（1905）。李格尔的观点给本雅明带来启发，即对艺术作品的解读应当考虑其生产的物质经济环境。

26. 罗纳德·里根（1911—2004），曾是美国电影演员，后成为共和党政治家，于 1981 至 1989 年任美国第 40 任总统。

27. 哥舒姆·舒勒姆（1897—1982），德国犹太裔历史学家、哲学家和犹太神秘主义学者，被视为卡巴拉学术研究的创始人之一。

28. 苏珊·桑塔格（1933—2004），美国犹太裔作家和政治活动家，代表作有《论摄影》（1977）、《疾病的隐喻》（1978）、《艾滋病及其隐喻》（1988）；并以一系列文集著称，例如《土星座下》（1980），其书名取自桑塔格评介瓦尔特·本雅明的同名文章，源于本雅明的自述。

29. 唐纳德·特朗普（1946 年生），地产大亨、电视明星，2017 年 1 月起任美国第 45 任总统。他在总统竞选中善用媒体公关，其言论也颇具民族主义色彩，因而一直被认为与 20 世纪 30 年代法西斯领袖极为相似。

30. 保罗·瓦雷里（1871—1945），法国诗人、散文家，法国象征主义诗歌运动代表人物。本雅明在《机械复制时代的艺术作品》中引用其谈论技术的论文《无处不在的征服》（1928）。

31. 弗吉尼亚·伍尔芙（1882—1941），被视为 20 世纪最有影响力、最重要的作家之一，代表作有《达洛维夫人》（1925）和散文《一间自己的房间》(1929)。伍尔芙的写作与"技术"关系密切，因而文学批评家运用本雅明的观点来分析其创作。

32. **古斯塔夫·维内肯**（1875—1964），德国教育改革家，其思想颇具影响力，但也饱受争议。他认为，青年组织的领导者不应是成年人，而应由较为年长的成员担任，这对德国青年运动意义深远（青年组织主要从事社会活动）。然而，维内肯还认为师生恋具有合理性，并于1921年与未成年人有过交往。瓦尔特·本雅明于1905至1907年在维内肯开办的寄宿学校念书，期间深受其政治观点的影响。

WAYS IN TO THE TEXT

KEY POINTS

- Walter Benjamin was a leftist German Jewish philosopher best known for "The Work of Art in the Age of Mechanical Reproduction"[1] and "Theses on the Philosophy of History."[2]

- "The Work of Art" examines the relationship between art, innovations in the technologies used to make art, and politics.

- The essay anticipated post-World War II* academic discussions concerning new media, culture, and politics.

Who Was Walter Benjamin?

Walter Benjamin was a German Jewish philosopher whose writings on capitalism's effects on art, politics, and social life remain vitally important today. Benjamin was born in Berlin in 1892 to an affluent household, but experienced poverty and hardship throughout much of his adult life. His early thought was influenced by the educational reformer Gustav Wyneken*, whom he met while a student at one of Wyneken's boarding schools. Wyneken was the editor of a radical* youth journal, *Der Anfang* (German for "The Beginning"), which was the voice of an intellectual youth movement devoted to the ideals of eighteenth- and nineteenth-century German philosophers, such as Hegel, Goethe, Kant, and Nietzsche.

Benjamin studied philosophy at the Universities of Freiburg, Berlin, Munich, and latterly Bern, where he received his PhD in 1919. While in Munich, he met the philosopher Gershom Scholem,* who became a lifelong friend, and who introduced him to Jewish mysticism.* His intellectual career took off in 1923, however, with the founding of the Institute for Social Research, where he met the

90

philosophers Theodor Adorno* and Georg Lukács,* whose works (particularly Lukács's 1920 book, *Theory of the Novel*) profoundly influenced his writing.

Benjamin wrote the first version of "The Work of Art" towards the end of 1935 while living in Paris, where he had been forced to move after the Nazis came to power and took away his German citizenship. A modified translation was published in French by the Institute for Social Research,* a hub for Marxist scholars that had moved from the University of Frankfurt to New York City due to fear of Nazi persecution. In an effort not to alienate a more pro-capitalist US audience, the editors omitted references to Karl Marx.* The version most frequently read today is the one Benjamin re-wrote in 1939, just as Europe was about to be torn apart by World War II and barely a year before Benjamin's suspected suicide while fleeing the Gestapo.* This version was not published in English until 1968.

What Does "The Work of Art" Say?

In "The Work of Art," Walter Benjamin argues that the concepts emphasized by traditional art criticism,* such as "creativity and genius, eternal value and mystery," are outdated. This is owing to two things: the emergence of new art forms, such as photography and film, which are viewed collectively and are experienced by the individual in different ways from painting or theatre; and the rise of fascism* across Europe, which relied on manipulating theatrical and artistic rhetoric to influence public opinion.

For Benjamin, an audience accustomed to film will be less

likely to be taken in by the spectacular displays used by fascist leaders to manipulate their opinions and draw attention away from social inequality. Film is a counter to what he calls the "aestheticization of politics,"* because it encourages distraction, which can be used in turn to ignore propaganda. Benjamin proposes a series of alternative concepts through which to understand art's reception in the age of these new technologies, and through which to identify art's revolutionary potential. The concepts he advances "differ from the more familiar terms [of art theory] in that they are completely useless for the purposes of fascism. They are, on the other hand, useful for the formulation of revolutionary demands in the politics of art."

For the fascists, Benjamin argues, audience reception of an artwork is fixed regardless of the place or time period in which it is viewed: thus, its value and meaning become unchangeable. Communists instead consider the network of forces at play in the social, cultural, and political conditions in which the artwork was produced, and they understand that an artwork's meaning and its reception changes in and through time, so that even its own past is subject to re-interpretation. For Benjamin, the work of art in the age of mechanical reproduction reveals how the past can be shaped in new ways by the present: film, for example, reconfigures the meaning of Shakespeare's plays in new ways that have an impact on the fixed words of the text. If the past is fluid, then so is the present. This in turn means that change is possible: Benjamin argues that we can transform the ways in which technology is organized, not only to produce art, but to oppose oppressive regimes.

While Benjamin's essay did not have much influence during his lifetime or during the first decades following its initial publication, it has had an enormous influence on art criticism, cultural studies, and literary theory since the late 1960s. The ideas set out in "The Work of Art" underpin John Berger's* influential work of art criticism, *Ways of Seeing* (1977), Susan Sontag's* study, *On Photography* (1977), and a wealth of literary and art criticism on twentieth-century literature and art as they relate to politics and technology. More recently, Benjamin's work has been mentioned alongside that of his fellow philosophers and friends Theodor Adorno and Max Horkheimer* in journalism covering the 2016 US presidential election, whose outcome some commentators have ascribed to Donald Trump's* manipulation of social media and reliance on a theatrical rhetoric devoid of actual content. Others have gone so far as to assert that Benjamin and his colleagues "knew Trump was coming"—a sensationalist claim that, however, helps explain the resurgence in public interest in their work.

Why Does "The Work of Art" Matter?

"The Work of Art" remains a seminal text for understanding the source of various arguments around the relationship between technological development, artistic production, politics, and public life that preoccupy scholars across the humanities and social sciences. Benjamin's identification of the effects that film and photography, including their mode of reception, could have on the public, and his recognition that medium matters as much as content, anticipated the ideas of later media theorists. His concern for the ways in which the reproducibility of an artwork might impinge upon our valuation of it, but also potentially democratize it and render audiences themselves participants, anticipated later discussions concerning the democratic potential of the Internet and user-generated content. Likewise, his hope that new media might enable a new form of art criticism capable of challenging the status quo will resonate with anyone who has followed the debate about the radical potential of blogging, Facebook, or Twitter.

"The Work of Art" also provides a useful path into engaging with Benjamin's work as a whole. A prolific writer, Benjamin wrote at length about history, politics, art, literature, religion, and, perhaps most famously, capitalism's effects on culture and society. The unorthodox nature of these texts, which move between disciplines and are written in an often maddeningly enigmatic style, makes them difficult to classify—but this is also the reason why Benjamin appeals to scholars working in such different fields. The fact that his ideas have been more widely influential on literary and cultural critics than on philosophers tells us something about their openness and applicability: in some ways, the society Benjamin writes about is not so removed from our own, globalized, digitized context, and the issues concerning art, technology, and power that he expresses remain relevant in the twenty-first century. Beyond academia, then, "The Work of Art" has relevance to anyone attempting to make sense of the polarization and fragmentation of political discourse today and the effects of new media and art on public life.

1. Walter Benjamin, "The Work of Art in the Age of Mechanical Reproduction", in *Illuminations*, ed. Hannah Arendt (London:Pimlico, 1999).

2. Walter Benjamin, "Theses on the Philosophy of History", in *Illuminations*, ed. Hannah Arendt (London: Pimlico, 1999).

SECTION 1
INFLUENCES

MODULE 1
THE AUTHOR AND THE HISTORICAL CONTEXT

KEY POINTS

- "The Work of Art in the Age of Mechanical Reproduction" is a seminal essay in the history of art criticism, literary studies* and critical theory.*

- Walter Benjamin was a leftist Jewish intellectual whose importance was only recognized several decades after his death.

- Benjamin's essay is a product of the tense years preceding World War II.

Why Read This Text?

In his influential essay, "The Work of Art in the Age of Mechanical Reproduction," the philosopher and cultural critic Walter Benjamin introduces a new set of concepts for understanding the art object in the modern era. Reconfiguring the traditional perspectives of art history* and art criticism, Benjamin argues that the work of art must be understood in relation to the material history of its production (how it came to be made) and in relation to the new ways in which audiences receive it. Benjamin identifies the significance of the emergent forms of photography and film, which allow for works of art to be reproduced and disseminated, and which audiences often experience collectively, and in a fundamentally different way from a painting or a play.

Benjamin argues that reproducibility erodes the "aura"* of

artworks: rather than existing in a separate, autonomous sphere (as art historians of the day argued), the work of art in the age of mechanical reproduction is part of everyday life. This is important because the view of art as autonomous,* according to Benjamin, has much in common with fascist rhetoric, which similarly relies on imposing one singular view, upholding social inequality as "natural," and treating life itself as a fixed and unchanging work of art. By contrast, understanding works of art as both a product of political circumstance and capable of shifting it, allows us to recognize art's revolutionary potential. While it went largely ignored for the first three decades following its publication, Benjamin's essay has greatly influenced literary and art criticism and cultural studies* since the 1970s, and has frequently been cited since the beginning of 2016 by journalists responding to the US presidential election and rise of right-wing extremism.[1]

> The pleasure [Benjamin] took in the physical act of writing … was as great as his aversion to mechanical expedients: in this respect the essay 'The Work of Art in the Age of Mechanical Reproduction,' like many other stages of his intellectual biography, was an act of identification with the aggressor.
>
> ——Theodor Adorno, "Benjamin the Letter Writer"

Author's Life

Walter Benjamin (1892–1940) was a leftist German Jewish philosopher born to an affluent family in Berlin. His father was a banker and an art dealer, who intended that his wealth would support Benjamin throughout adulthood so he would not have to secure paid work. As Hannah Arendt* has noted, this socio-economic privilege was characteristic of an entire generation of German-Jewish intellectuals born at the end of the nineteenth century, whose parents supported them financially so that they could study and write.[2] This wealth contrasted sharply with the poverty Benjamin experienced in later life. The economic depression in Germany following World War I* (also known as the Great Depression*) rendered his father unable to financially support him and his wife, Dora Sophie Pollak.* Benjamin thus struggled in the following decades to find ways to get paid for his writing.[3] These financial struggles also affected his marriage, which lasted only eleven years: he and Dora had a son in 1918, but separated in 1928.

Benjamin spent the years of World War I translating writings of the poet Charles Baudelaire,* which indelibly influenced his interest in the relationship between capitalism,* urbanization,* and art—as manifest in essays such as "Paris, Capital of the Nineteenth Century" (1935; 1939), and "On Some Motifs in Baudelaire." The latter essay was intended to form part of his unfinished magnum opus, *The Arcades Project* (1927–),* a study of the Paris shopping arcades.* Benjamin's translations of Baudelaire were published as *Charles Baudelaire, Tableaux Parisiens* (1923).*

Author's Background

"The Work of Art" is an anti-fascist essay composed during fascism's ascent. In February 1933, the Reichstag,* the building that housed the German Parliament, was set ablaze. The recently elected Chancellor, the anti-Semitic,* anti-communist, and fiercely nationalist politician Adolf Hitler,* used the burning of the Reichstag to pass emergency measures that removed communist opposition (the fire was alleged to have been started by communist insurgents) and ultimately consolidated power for his National Socialist German Workers' Party,* also known as the Nazis, by making them the majority. Paying heed to the increasing violence surrounding this political shift, Benjamin went into exile in March 1933, spending most of the 1930s living in Paris when he had the necessary funds. He also traveled extensively around Europe, often staying with friends and acquaintances in order to fund his writing. He wrote both versions of "The Work of Art" while in Paris—the first in 1935, and the final version in 1939, just after the Nazis had taken away his German citizenship.[4]

The Nazi invasion of France in 1940, and the Gestapo's subsequent confiscation of Benjamin's vast personal library and a number of his unfinished manuscripts, forced him to flee France. He left his notes for the book he was writing at the time, *The Arcades Project*, with the writer Georges Bataille,* who was librarian at the Bibliothèque nationale de France. Benjamin's plan was to cross the Franco-Spanish border at Portbou, use a Spanish transit visa to travel from Spain to Lisbon, and from there board a ship to the United States, using an emergency visa issued to him as a German refugee in Marseilles by the United States government. A series of misfortunes rendered this plan unfeasible. Thus, on the night of September 26, 1940, upon discovering that the Spanish police were not honoring visas made out in Marseilles, he allegedly committed suicide. Ironically, this act made an impression on the border officials, who allowed his fellow travelers to cross into Spain after all, and within a few weeks the visa embargo was lifted.[5] The very real threat of fascism that Benjamin's generation faced, and that ultimately took his life, forms an important backdrop to "The Work of Art."

1. Tom Whyman, "Which Philosophy Can Best Explain 2016?", *Vice*, December 15, 2016, accessed June 20, 2017, https://www.vice.com/en_uk/article/ z4ngy4/which-philosophy-can-help-us-understand-2016; Jeremy Roos, "Trump's victory speaks to a crumbling liberal order", *Roar*, November 9, 2016, accessed June 20, 2017, https://roarmag.org/essays/trump-victory- legitimation-crisis-capitalism/; Stuart Jeffries, "Why a forgotten 1930s critique of capitalism is back in fashion", *Guardian*, September 9, 2016, accessed June 20, 2017, https://www.theguardian.com/books/2016/ sep/09/marxist-critique-capitalism-frankfurt-school-cultural-apocalypse; Alex Ross, "The Frankfurt School Knew Trump Was Coming", *New Yorker*, December 5, 2016, accessed June 20, 2017, http://www.newyorker.com/culture/cultural-comment/the-frankfurt-school-knew-trump-was-coming.

2. Hannah Arendt, "Introduction: Walter Benjamin, 1892–1940" (1968), in Illuminations, trans. Harry Zohn and ed. Hannah Arendt (London: Pimlico, 1999 [1970]), 7–60 (31).

3. Howard Eiland and Michael W. Jennings, *Walter Benjamin: A Critical Life* (Cambridge, MA: Belknap Press/Harvard University Press, 2013), 3; 221; 412.

4. Rolf Goebel, "Introduction: Benjamin's Actuality", in *A Companion to the Works of Walter Benjamin*, ed. Rolf Goebel (London: Camden House, 2009), 1–22 (6).

5. Arendt, "Introduction: Walter Benjamin, 1892–1940", 23.

MODULE 2
ACADEMIC CONTEXT

KEY POINTS

* Walter Benjamin's "The Work of Art in the Age of Mechanical Reproduction" draws on Western Marxism,* Surrealism,* and Dada* while refuting Futurism.*
* While a number of Benjamin's colleagues sought to challenge fascism and capitalist ideology, not all of these scholars shared Benjamin's optimism about mass culture.*
* The philosophers Theodor Adorno and Max Horkheimer and the playwright Bertolt Brecht* were among Benjamin's greatest influences.

The Work in Its Context

"The Work of Art" is very difficult to categorize, as it incorporates ideas from a range of disciplines to challenge the very terms by which art, politics, and culture should be discussed. However, Western Marxism,* Dada, Surrealism, and Futurism loom largest in the text.

Building on the work of political theorist Karl Marx, Marxist critics approach cultural phenomena in relation to the material conditions that produce them. They are concerned by the ways in which capitalism mediates our relationship with the people, places and things around us. Expanding upon Marx's idea of commodity fetishism*[1]—that human relations under capitalism become transactional—Georg Lukács argued that under capitalism, objects are valued over and above the people who made them.[2] Benjamin's essay extends Lukács's ideas, but differs in its identification of the radical possibilities that the loss of the artwork's aura opens up.

Surrealism and Dada were two related movements in literature and the visual arts that Benjamin wrote about at length throughout the 1920s,[3] and which were greatly influenced by Marxist thought. These artists sought to create works that would scandalize viewers, shocking them out of their daily routines and forcing them to reassess what they knew. They did this to challenge capitalist culture, which, like their Marxist critic contemporaries, they saw as creating a population of sleepwalking consumer-citizens disincentivized from questioning their political leaders or the lifestyle imposed on them. Benjamin explicitly mentions Dada's shock tactics in his essay, seeing them as the precursor to the special effects afforded by film.

Futurism was an artistic movement that developed in Italy around the same time as Surrealism and Dada. However, where the former two aligned themselves with socialist* views, the latter championed nationalism,* fascism, and violence. In particular, Futurists saw speed, technology, and capitalist progress as means to make Italy a leader on the global stage. They famously called war "the world's only hygiene"[4]—change could only be brought about through the destruction of past traditions by violent means. When Benjamin challenges the "aestheticization of politics"—the use of pageantry and spectacle to make the masses feel allegiance to the nation state and ignore their own suffering—he is also challenging Futurism's celebration of these methods.

> The history of every art form shows critical epochs in which
> a certain art form aspires to effects which could be fully
> obtained only with a changed technical standard ... Dadaism
> attempted to create by pictorial—and literary—means the
> effects which the public today seeks in the film.
>
> ——Walter Benjamin, "The Work of Art in the
> Age of Mechanical Reproduction"

Overview of the Field

While his approach was innovative, Benjamin was not alone in challenging the rise of fascism or capitalism's effects on culture. Rather, he formed part of a group of anti-fascist Marxist scholars working at the Institute for Social Research led by Max Horkheimer and Theodor Adorno. Scholars associated with the Institute for Social Research are referred to today as the "Frankfurt School,"* after the University of Frankfurt, where it was originally based. The Institute moved to New York City in 1934 to escape Nazi persecution. As well as publishing "The Work of Art," the Institute funded some of Benjamin's other work.

Perhaps the best-known work to emerge from the Frankfurt School is Adorno and Horkheimer's *Dialectic of Enlightenment: Philosophical Fragments* (1947). One of the essays in this collection, "The Culture Industry: Enlightenment as Mass Deception,"* examines similar themes to Benjamin's "The Work of Art," but argues that popular culture renders people passive consumers rather than critically and politically engaged citizens. Popular film and fiction simply recycles the same themes and storylines over and over again, since tried-and-tested formulae are guaranteed to make money. The end result is a society in which art is treated like a consumer product. This argument was very different from Benjamin's. Where Benjamin sees the new media of his day as a potential means to oppose fascism, Adorno sees no hope: photography and film, he argues, have already been co-opted* to lull citizens into submission. Film doesn't shock viewers into recognizing they are oppressed: rather, it offers an escape from reality that in turn serves the needs of capitalism, since viewers return home from the movies satisfied and once again willing to accept the status quo. While the essay collection was published after Benjamin's death, Adorno expressed some of these ideas in his letters to Benjamin, where he also criticized "The Work of Art" as overly optimistic.[5]

Academic Influences

The ideas of the Marxist German playwright Bertolt Brecht, whom Benjamin met in the late 1920s, were also highly influential on Benjamin's work. In Hannah Arendt's words, Benjamin saw Brecht as "the poet who was most at home in this [the twentieth] century."[6] For Benjamin, Brecht exemplified what was needed of artists at the time: "A total absence of illusion about the age and at the same time an unlimited commitment to it."[7] By this he meant that Brecht was at once aware of the severity of the rise of fascism and the threats of unchecked capitalism, and committed to fighting these—virtues that Benjamin celebrates in "The Work of Art."

Benjamin wrote about Brecht in a series of essays that were

only published posthumously in 1966. Here he identified the significance of the "standstill"*: a moment in Brecht's theatrical productions when the actions are interrupted, thus forcing the audience to "take up a position"[8] by "expos[ing] the present" and "alienating [them] in a lasting manner, through thought, from the conditions in which [they] liv[e]."[9] In "The Work of Art," Benjamin likewise expresses the need for art that will make us critically reflect, but without falling into the trap of self-absorbed contemplation.

Finally, Benjamin was influenced by the work of the late-nineteenth-century Austrian art historian Alois Riegl,* and particularly by the methods that Riegl used in his book, *Late Roman Art Industry* (1905).* For Benjamin, Riegl's work stood out in its recognition that the characteristics of the marketplace in which an artist was operating needed to be addressed alongside more conventional aesthetic concerns, such as genre* or technique.*[10] Because he was more interested in the conditions of artistic production, Riegl paid attention to works of art that usually had been neglected by art historians, but which he identified as important cultural artifacts. This alternative emphasis forms a pivotal component of Benjamin's essay.

---

1. Karl Marx, "The fetishism of commodities and the secret there of", *Capital: An abridged edition*, ed. David McLellan (Oxford: Oxford University Press, 2008 [1867]), 42–50.

2. Georg Lukács, *History and Class Consciousness: Studies in Marxist Dialectics* (London: Merlin, 1968 [1923]), 83.

3. Walter Benjamin, "Surrealism" (1929), reprinted in *One-Way Street and Other Writings*, ed. Amit Chaudhuri and trans. J. A. Underwood (London: Penguin, 2009), 143–160; Walter Benjamin, "Dream Kitsch: Gloss on Surrealism" (1925), reprinted in *The Work of Art in the Age of Its Technical Reproducibility and Other Writings*, ed. Michael W. Jennings et al, trans. Edmund Jephcott, Rodney Livingstone, Howard Eiland et al. (Cambridge, MA: Belknap/Harvard University Press, 2008), 236–239.

4. Tommaso Marinetti, "Futurist Manifesto" (1908), in *Theories of Modern Art: A Source Book by Artists and Critics*, ed. Herschel B. Chipp (Berkeley, CA: University of California Press, 1996 [1968]), 285–287(286).

5. Theodor W. Adorno and Walter Benjamin, *The Complete Correspondence: 1928–1940*, trans. Nicholas Walker (Cambridge: Polity, 1999), 127–134.

6. Erdmut Wizislda, *Walter Benjamin and Bertolt Brecht: The Story of a Friendship*, trans. Christine Shuttleworth (New Haven: Yale University Press), 103.

7. Wizislda, *Walter Benjamin and Bertolt Brecht*, 103.

8. Walter Benjamin, *Understanding Brecht*, trans. Anna Bostock (London: Verso, 1998), 100.

9. Benjamin, *Understanding Brecht*, 100.

10. T. Y. Levin, "Walter Benjamin and the Theory of Art History", *October* 47 (Winter 1988), 77–83; Mike Gubster, *Time's Visible Surface: Alois Riegl and the Discourse on History and Temporality in Fin-de-Siécle Vienna* (Detroit, MI: Wayne State University Press, 2006), 20; 202; 208–212.

MODULE 3
THE PROBLEM

KEY POINTS

- Walter Benjamin's "The Work of Art in the Age of Mechanical Reproduction" investigates the political ramifications of the processes of technological reproduction.*
- "The Work of Art" challenges received ideas about art's autonomy, while building on the work of Marxist critics.
- Benjamin argues that the idealized view of art as unchanging and everlasting can be easily manipulated to uphold the status quo.

Core Question

In what ways do the processes of technological reproduction available in the first decades of the twentieth century alter the production and reception of works of art? What are the political consequences of these altered states?

While fascism was very much at the forefront of public and scholarly debate during this politically charged period, the questions Benjamin addresses in "The Work of Art" were not. His essay was therefore highly original. Benjamin attempts to address these questions by analyzing the changing status of what he terms the "aura" that surrounds works of art through an exploration of the relationship of that aura to technology and the historical context. "That which withers in the age of mechanical reproduction is the aura of the work of art," he argues.[1]

While Benjamin does not explicitly define the "aura," the essay makes clear that it is connected to art's historical association with the rituals of the church or monarchy (what Benjamin calls its "cult" value), and to the ideas of authenticity and autonomy that have been traditionally attributed to great art works. When a work of art can be reproduced in a book or as a postcard, the uniqueness of its location as an object occupying one specific place that people travel from far and wide to visit is undermined. Reproduction allows the work of art in the modern age to be re-appropriated—pinned to a bedroom wall, sent to a distant relative, juxtaposed with advertisements for coffee. This capacity for reproduction has a democratizing effect. More than this, new technologies have delivered new art forms, such as film and photography, that no longer require a unique or original object. There is no "original" film reel or photograph: all copies are equal.

> *Earlier much futile thought had been devoted to the question of whether photography is an art. The primary question—whether the very invention of photography had not transformed the entire nature of art—was not raised.*
>
> —— Walter Benjamin, "The Work of Art in the Age of Mechanical Reproduction"

The Participants

Benjamin's essay engages with two sets of received ideas. First, it challenges the idea of the work of art that was still dominant in traditional art criticism, where the work of art was studied as an autonomous object located in a separate sphere from the material realities of the everyday world. While capable of reflecting the context in which it was created, such an object was considered to qualify as a work of art thanks to its uniqueness, which allowed it to *transcend* that context. It was as if it contained some transmissible kernel of eternal and unchanging value that also reflected its authenticity and uniqueness. The aura that this idea gave to the work of art isolated it from the subsequent contexts in which it was viewed and received.

The second set of received ideas is Western Marxism—a term coined by the philosopher Maurice Merleau-Ponty* to refer to elaborations of Marx's ideas in Western and Central Europe. Benjamin's essay offers a radical critique of capitalism as well as art history, for he identifies how concepts relating to how art has been traditionally viewed help to support capitalism and fascism. This approach, which concentrates on cultural production rather than the formal techniques of art, has much in common with other thinkers with whom Benjamin was in dialogue.

The Contemporary Debate

Benjamin's essay argues that the idealized versions of art upheld by traditional art history can easily be deployed to sustain and naturalize massive social inequalities. The persistence of separating art from its various contexts forms part of a wider process that enables the dominant culture to limit the possibility of changing the status quo. It also enables that dominant culture to incorporate and neutralize dissent.

Against the backdrop of an ascending fascism, Benjamin's essay reveals the potentially dire political consequences of defending a traditional notion of an art work as something authentic, autonomous, eternal, and unchanging: for these are the same terms the Nazis also used to justify their violence and oppression. For Benjamin, such a position aestheticizes politics: it allows leaders to dupe the public into thinking of the nation state itself as an unchanging and unchangeable work of art. He wants to reverse this to show how it is possible to instead politicize art and instigate radical political action on a mass scale.

Benjamin thus seeks to link the study of art to the wider social and cultural processes that impact upon its production (how it is made), reception (how it is viewed), and reproduction (how it is disseminated). Examining the work of art in relation to this wider context enables him to consider the critical limitations and political consequences of a more traditional approach. It also enables him to establish an innovative set of approaches to art history that reflect his engagement with the Marxist study of culture. Benjamin, however, diverges from fellow Marxist thinkers, such as Siegfried Kracauer* and Theodor Adorno, who viewed mass culture as a source of distraction that ultimately prevents citizens from engaging politically: instead, he sees it as holding the potential for radical change. Where Kracauer and Adorno view new media as further tools of capitalist exploitation, Benjamin argues that new media has the capacity to shock people into action.

---

1. Walter Benjamin, "The Work of Art in the Age of Mechanical Reproduction", in *Illuminations*, ed. Hannah Arendt (London: Pimlico, 1999), 215.

MODULE 4
THE AUTHOR'S CONTRIBUTION

KEY POINTS

* "The Work of Art in the Age of Mechanical Reproduction" formulates a theory of art criticism that cannot be co-opted by fascism, and might be used to instigate social change.
* The advent of new media and changes in art's reception are transforming the public's perception of art and communication.
* Benjamin's unique argument involves appropriating quotes from previous sources in a process resembling collage* or montage.*

Author's Aims

Walter Benjamin's "The Work of Art in the Age of Mechanical Reproduction" was purposefully designed to combat fascism, or, at least, to formulate a way of critiquing, and thinking about, modern art that could not be co-opted by fascists. The need for such a work had become increasingly apparent as the ruling Nazi party in Germany deployed fascist policies that suppressed civil liberties and persecuted specific sections of the population, primarily the large and diverse Jewish community that included Benjamin's family. Benjamin's analysis of the work of art in an age of new technologies of production, reception, and reproduction, is thus an attempt to identify ways in which the art generated by new technologies might serve the interests of those alienated and oppressed by the dominant regimes of capitalism and right-wing extremism in the Western world, be this by enabling outright revolution or by opening up more democratic ways of thinking about art and culture as a whole.

Benjamin's optimism regarding the radical potential of mass culture (namely film, but also photography, magazines, and popular fiction) was dramatically different from that of his fellow Marxist scholars, and indeed from that of more conservative art critics of the period. Those associated with the Frankfurt School thought that mass culture promoted passivity—a population of distracted, uncritical consumer-viewers switched off from politics—and could be used to control public opinion. Conservative art critics instead saw it as killing the intellect and imagination: they urged their middle-class readers to stay away from the "trash" consumed by the lower classes. Art critics further perceived these new forms as taking away their own authority as experts: as Benjamin himself notes, "it is inherent in the technique of the film as well as that of sports that everybody who witnesses its accomplishments is somewhat of an expert."[1] They viewed this leveling of the playing field as a threat. Benjamin's essay was thus original both in its analysis of reproducibility and in his optimistic view of its ramifications.

During long periods of history, the mode of human sense perception changes with humanity's entire mode of existence. The manner in which human sense perception is organized, the medium in which it is accomplished, is determined not only by nature but by historical circumstances as well."

——Walter Benjamin, "The Work of Art in the Age of Mechanical Reproduction"

Approach

Benjamin's unusual approach involves setting out a series of ideas in fourteen distinct "theses,"* or condensed mini-essays, in which he analyses not only the history of artistic reproduction and the erosion of the art object's "aura," but also specific technical features of photography and film, the changing relationship between audience and medium, and the radical potential of distraction. The essay thus unspools as a series of different arguments that together show connections between the specific characteristics of the new media he is discussing, and a broader shift in the public's relationship to art and rhetoric* (the ways in which messages are expressed). The originality of this argument lies in the fact that for Benjamin, the very features of photograph and film that render them inauthentic forms will, in turn, change the public's reception of *all* forms of performance and expression—not only painting, music, or theater, but also the speeches, parades, and other public displays mounted by fascist leaders to instill allegiance to the state. Benjamin argues that exposure to new media will result in a new skepticism towards aesthetics (art and display) as a whole, leading people to recognize when spectacle is being used by their leaders to manipulate public opinion. Thus, for Benjamin, the erosion of traditional artworks' authority following the advent of new media, and the shifts in public reception of artworks, have the potential to bring about new forms of opposition to fascism. Such a view was unprecedented.

Contribution in Context

While a highly original essay, "The Work of Art" bears the imprint of numerous thinkers. This is attested in the essay's famous first line, "When Marx undertook his critique of the capitalistic mode of production,* this mode was in its infancy,"[2] as well as in the many citations of writers, philosophers, and critics. As in Benjamin's other work, the reference to Marx and proliferation of quotes from other texts aims to situate his argument within Marxist discourse as well as to respond to debates in art and literary criticism occurring at the time. Thus, for example, the essay's epigraph (the quote that comes before the opening sentence) is from French poet and essayist Paul Valéry's* (1871–1945) essay, "The Conquest of Ubiquity" (1928),* in which Valéry speculates about the likely effects of new technologies on culture at large.[3]

Benjamin later quotes another passage from this same essay:"Just as water, gas, and electricity are brought into our houses from far off to satisfy our needs in response to a minimal effort, so we shall be supplied with visual or auditory images, which will appear and disappear at a simple movement of the hand, hardly more than a sign."[4] However, where Valéry's text is referring to the rapidity with which technology is likely to transform people's lives beyond the point of recognition, Benjamin uses the passage to support his view that traditional art forms anticipate the new technologies that follow.

This method of attributing new meaning to other writers' words is characteristic of Benjamin, who does not quote other writers in order to adopt their arguments, but instead interprets their words in new ways that ultimately serve his own, often very different, viewpoint. This approach resembles the techniques of visual collage and cinematic and literary montage in which Benjamin was so interested. Both forms involve juxtaposing fragments of (usually unrelated) material from different sources to create new meanings. Readers today may in turn find themselves interpreting these de-contextualised quotes somewhat differently— for example, the quote from Valéry's essay seems to eerily predict the advent of the Internet.

---

1. Walter Benjamin, "The Work of Art in the Age of Mechanical Reproduction", in *Illuminations*, ed. Hannah Arendt (London: Pimlico, 1999), 225.
2. Benjamin, "The Work of Art", 211.
3. Paul Valéry, "The Conquest of Ubiquity" (1928), in *Aesthetics*, trans. Ralph Manheim (New York: Pantheon Books, 1964), 226, quoted in "The Work of Art", 211.

SECTION 2
IDEAS

MAIN IDEAS

KEY POINTS

* "The Work of Art in the Age of Mechanical Reproduction" is concerned with the effects that new technologies enabling artworks to be reproduced are having on society.

* Benjamin shows how reproducibility renders art more accessible, challenges traditional art criticism, and can instigate political change.

* Benjamin's fragmentary writing style is in keeping with the nonconformist approach to criticism he is promoting.

Key Themes

The main themes in Benjamin's essay involve the relationships between the work of art, technologies of reproduction, and political change. Technological changes that enable multiple copies of an art work to be reproduced challenge traditional notions of the work of art as an autonomous object imbued with an "aura" of authenticity and unchanging value. Benjamin argues that with the mass dissemination of images, the "aura" attached to the work of art is eroded. Disconnected from church and monarchy, and rendered more widely available, the work of art is democratized.

Benjamin connects this argument to a longer historical shift, from the work of art's status as a ritual object—either through magic, religion, or as an object of beauty to be passively contemplated—to its new status: as a political object. Benjamin outlines a related shift within this historical perspective as the artwork changes from having cult value (as a ritual object) to exhibition value (as an object to be showcased). In the modern era, he argues, art will be used to either manipulate the masses into submission or enable their liberation.

For Benjamin, film and photography have affected the ways in which we perceive and experience the world, and have the capacity to challenge oppressive regimes. This is because film's obvious lack of authenticity—the fact that there is nothing to distinguish a film's "original" reel from its copies, and that the medium itself is in fact designed for reproduction and dissemination—renders audiences more aware of other artificial displays, such as the parades that totalitarian leaders use to dupe the public into submission (what Benjamin calls the "aestheticization of politics"). According to Benjamin, the differences in how audiences watch film compared to traditional art forms will affect how they experience other forms of display, including propaganda: "The public is an examiner, but an absent-minded one."[1]

> [T]he instant the criterion of authenticity ceases to be applicable to artistic production, the total function of art is reversed. Instead of being based on ritual, it begins to be based on another practice—politics.
>
> —— Walter Benjamin, "The Work of Art in the Age of Mechanical Reproduction"

Exploring the Ideas

Benjamin explores the idea of the "aura" in Theses One and Two of his essay. While all art is reproducible, an imitation of a painting does not erode the original's authority since it can easily be revealed to be a fake. Technological reproductions, by contrast, can exist independently to the original: first, by using close ups to bring out details not immediately evident in the original, and second, by enabling the original to be shared elsewhere.[2]

As well as resulting in the aura's depreciation, these characteristics will inevitably change people's perception of the world around them. In fact, Benjamin argues, film will change "humanity's entire mode of existence"[3] and for this reason it is the pre-eminent "mode of human sense perception" of the twentieth century.[4] Its most influential aspects are its mass reception (people watch films collectively, and the movie industry reaches far more members of the public than gallery exhibitions can), and the possibilities it allows for audiences to see the world around them in far sharper focus.

Theses Four and Five introduce the outmodedness of "Art for Art's Sake"*: the idea that art should be revered uncritically, and considered to be elevated above its spectators, which Benjamin argues preserves art's ritual function. Reproducibility injects political meaning into artwork, Benjamin contends. Eugène Atget's* photographs in the 1900s, for example, were used in magazine and newspaper articles as "standard evidence for historical occurrences," in turn "acquir[ing] a political significance."[5]

Benjamin also notes that film, like the newspaper, allows for audience participation, which causes "the distinction between author and public … to lose its basic character."[6] More specifically:

"Any man today can lay claim to being filmed;"[7] likewise,"today there is hardly a gainfully employed European who could not, in principle, find an opportunity to publish somewhere or other."[8] Benjamin's concern here is not, however, with the potential for photography or film to communicate radical ideas (which he notes can be co-opted by the companies that publish or produce them), so much as for the potential for "a revolutionary criticism of traditional concepts of art."[9] While these new forms themselves may not be able to instigate social change, they can help dismantle old ways of understanding art that risk upholding oppressive social structures.

Finally, and most contentiously, Benjamin proposes that new media's alleged diminishing of the viewing public's attention span and capacity to absorb information should be seen as a good thing. Distraction* is a way to ignore the many stimuli of mass culture (advertising billboards, shop window displays, tabloid newspaper headlines) and preserve one's energy to attend to important content and political action. The distraction triggered by moving pictures is a way to counteract capitalist culture's imposition on the individual's mental energies, and should be seen as a tool for good.

Language and Expression

Benjamin's friend and collaborator Theodor Adorno, wrote that Benjamin was the "unsurpassed master" at a form of essay writing in which each theme builds upon its predecessor to construct a coherent argument.[10] Adorno clarifies his statement by explaining that in such essays, thought "does not progress in a single direction; instead, the moments are interwoven as in a carpet. The fruitfulness of the thoughts depends on the density of the texture."[11] Elsewhere, Adorno commented that Benjamin's "philosophy of fragmentation remained itself fragmentary," a victim of its preferred method. For Adorno, that method "cannot be separated from its content."[12]

This fragmented approach is apparent in "The Work of Art," which is divided into fourteen separate theses, a prologue and an epilogue—an approach that prevents the reader from differentiating between the form of his work (its literary features) and its content (what it says). This is important because Benjamin himself views the distinction between form and content to be both old-fashioned and politically suspect: the two must be examined in conjunction with each other. Benjamin's unorthodox argument thus finds an equivalent in the unorthodox style of the text itself, which does not propose a single, coherent, and overarching point, but rather various loosely connected ideas. This style in turn prevents the reader from drawing final conclusions, which is one reason why Benjamin's work continues to be discussed.

---

1. Walter Benjamin, "The Work of Art in the Age of Mechanical Reproduction", in *Illuminations*, ed. Hannah Arendt (London: Pimlico, 1999), 234.
2. Benjamin, "The Work of Art," 214.
3. Benjamin, "The Work of Art," 216.
4. Benjamin, "The Work of Art," 216.
5. Benjamin, "The Work of Art," 220.
6. Benjamin, "The Work of Art," 225.
7. Benjamin, "The Work of Art," 225.

8. Benjamin, "The Work of Art," 225.

9. Benjamin, "The Work of Art," 224.

10. Theodor W. Adorno, "The Essay as Form", in *Notes to Literature: Volume One*, trans. Shierry Weber Nicholsen (New York: Columbia University, 1991), 3–23 (13).

11. Adorno, "The Essay as Form," 13.

12. Theodor W. Adorno, "A Portrait of Walter Benjamin", in *Prisms*, trans. Samuel and Shierry Weber (Cambridge, MA: MIT, 1988), 227–242 (239).

MODULE 6
SECONDARY IDEAS

KEY POINTS

* "The Work of Art in the Age of Mechanical Reproduction" also examines the effects of photography, film, and technological innovation more broadly on our perception of the world around us.

* Benjamin shows how the camera alters the relationship between actor and audience, reveals aspects of the world hitherto hidden, and is at once absorbing and immersive, and yet experienced distractedly.

* While Benjamin intended his essay to be a political critique, it has largely been read as a work of art criticism: thus, his central points have also been the most overlooked.

Other Ideas

While the "The Work of Art in the Age of Mechanical Reproduction" is, at heart, about how art criticism might be used to resist fascism, it is also a study of the transformative effects of specific techniques in film and photography on our perception of the world around us—and a meditation on technology itself. While these points are secondary to Benjamin's concepts of the aura, politicized art, and aestheticized politics, they are nevertheless important for an exhaustive understanding of both the essay and his broader body of work. Of particular note are his examination of the camera's mediation of the traditional relationship between actor and audience; his assessment of its revelation of aspects of the world that would otherwise remain hidden; and his contention that the collective viewing aspect makes spectators more amenable to experimental films than they would be to experimental paintings, which are viewed singly and by a middle- class demographic that still responds to the authority of art critics.

In Thesis Seven, Benjamin notes that when photography first emerged, critics were concerned with "whether photography was an art. The primary question—whether the very invention of photography had not transformed the entire nature of art—was not raised."[1] His essay thus broaches this transformation.

> Unmistakably, reproduction as offered by picture magazines and newsreels differs from the image seen by the unarmed eye. Uniqueness and permanence are as closely linked in the latter as are transitoriness and reproducibility in the former.
>
> —— Walter Benjamin, "The Work of Art in the Age of Mechanical Reproduction"

Exploring the Ideas

Film, Benjamin argues, has transformed the traditional relationship between actor and audience by the use of the camera. The camera manipulates the appearance of the actors and their actions by changing angles and through the use of close-ups, while the actions themselves are often filmed in stages and only assembled later: all of this creates distance between audience and actors. "The audience's identification with the actor is really an identification with the camera."[2] Likewise, since film actors do not perform for people sitting in front of them, whose responses might alter their performance from one show to the next, the relationship between the cast and viewers is more like that between a shelf of consumer goods and their eventual buyers. During shooting, "the actor has as little contact with [the audience] as any article made in a factory."[3]

At the same time, however, film allows for the examination of minutiae—details in the landscape, in a person's gait, or the sound of a faucet dripping—that we would not be able to perceive otherwise. He compares this ability to isolate details to the skills of the psychoanalyst. Psychoanalysis* contends that an individual's life is composed of both their conscious thoughts and actions, and the hundreds and thousands of impulses, desires, and aversions of which they are completely unaware because they occur subconsciously. Like the psychoanalyst with the individual's mind, film reveals aspects of the world of which we were not conscious before. The ability to slow down or speed up a filmed sequence affords us a completely new understanding of the subject captured. "The camera introduces us to unconscious optics as does psychoanalysis to unconscious impulses."[4]

Likewise, film affords an immersive experience: comparing the painter to a magician, the cameraman to a surgeon, and reality to a sick body undergoing treatment, Benjamin notes in Thesis Eleven that the painter, like the magician moving his hands over a sick body without touching it, remains at a "natural distance from reality," while the cameraman, like the surgeon cutting into the body, "penetrates deeply" into it.[5]

Elsewhere, Benjamin makes a comparison between film's

immersive quality, which the audience experiences distractedly, with that of architecture. This connects to a broader point about the time lag between the most advanced artistic practices and technology. Art, he argues, anticipates shifts that subsequent technologies will make more widespread and more mainstream: "just as lithography virtually implied the illustrated newspaper, so did photography foreshadow the sound film."[6] By the same token, a city dweller's distracted experience of architecture, which they move through without properly observing, is akin to that of the movie-going public, who is "an examiner, but an absent-minded one."[7]

Such points indirectly feed back into the main themes of Benjamin's essay in relation to the effect of technological reproducibility on the production and reception of the work of art, and on modern experience and perception more generally.

Overlooked

The political dimension of Benjamin's argument was marginalized for many years. The history of the different versions of the essay emphasizes this point. Benjamin's references to Marx and his explicit subscription to socialism and opposition to fascism were initially suppressed. However, even the most popular English-language version of the essay—a version that includes these references—has, in the words of Benjamin scholar Susan Buck-Morss,* been "read, in the United States at least, as a thoroughly depoliticized* defense of the culture industry" rather than an attempt to use mass culture to oppose totalitarianism.*[8] Benjamin's essay, Morss argues, is a manifesto of political aesthetics:* it demonstrates how any discussion of art is already political. To ignore the political dimension of Benjamin's argument is to miss the whole point of the essay.

Approaching Benjamin's essay as a political manifesto in turn makes it easier to see the connections between it and other important essays he wrote, such as "The Author as Producer"* and "Theses on the Philosophy of History,"* which seek to reveal the political dimension of cultural production (in this case, artistic production and the writing of history).

Beyond this glaring omission, however, Benjamin's essay has been thoroughly mined by scholars both within Benjamin studies and in other disciplines, who have eagerly applied its ideas in the discussion of new and emergent technologies. One might even argue—as Morss does in the above-mentioned speech—that Benjamin's essay has been *overly* used, often at the cost of diluting its original ideas.

1. Walter Benjamin, "The Work of Art in the Age of Mechanical Reproduction", in *Illuminations*, ed. Hannah Arendt (London: Pimlico, 1999), 220.
2. Benjamin, "The Work of Art", 222.
3. Benjamin, "The Work of Art", 224.
4. Benjamin, "The Work of Art", 230.
5. Benjamin, "The Work of Art", 227.
6. Benjamin, "The Work of Art", 213.

7. Benjamin, "The Work of Art", 234.

8. Susan Buck-Morss, "Anti-Stalinist Art: Benjamin, Shostakovich, and the End of the Story", Keynote lecture of the first Congress of the International Walter Benjamin Association, Amsterdam, July 1997. Published as "Revolutionary Time: The Vanguard and the Avant-Garde", in *Benjamin Studies*, Studien 1, ed. Helga Geyer Ryan (Amsterdam: Rodopi, 2002), accessed July 13, 2017, http://susanbuckmorss.info/text/antistalinist-art/.

MODULE 7

ACHIEVEMENT

KEY POINTS

* "The Work of Art in the Age of Mechanical Reproduction" is a highly influential essay despite its overly optimistic assessment of mass culture and new media.

* Benjamin's essay engaged in original ways with contemporary debates around the status of film and photography and the rise of fascism.

* "The Work of Art" failed to anticipate how the art market would eventually commercialize the aura of authenticity of artworks.

Assessing the Argument

As the title of Benjamin's essay intimates, "The Work of Art in the Age of Mechanical Reproduction" puts as much emphasis on technology as the work of art. Benjamin's essay traces the origins of transformations and changes in perception in the modern era to new techniques and creative practices. At this level, the essay has proved to have an unexpected relevance for a digital age in which new technologies—computers, the Internet, mobile phones—have fundamentally altered the way we interact with the world (as well as on the technologically inflected ways that artists produce their work).[1]

However, Benjamin's emphasis on film as the key revolutionary medium driving this cultural shift has proved romantically optimistic given the spectacularly reactionary* and formulaic quality of mainstream cinema. The manufactured aura around the film star that he identifies in his essay perpetuates the same kind of separation between the audience and performer that Benjamin hoped would be countered by the potentially liberating techniques of montage (whereby the story is told through the juxtaposition of short, segmented clips) and other optical effects. These effects have, instead, failed to jolt the viewer from a passive contemplation of a seemingly unchanging and unchangeable system into engaging in a more active transformation of the world.[2]

> [F]or the first time in world history, mechanical reproduction emancipates the work of art from its parasitical dependence on ritual. To an ever greater degree the work of art reproduced becomes the work of art designed for reproducibility. From a photographic negative, for example, one can make any number of prints; to ask for the 'authentic' print makes no sense.
>
> —— Walter Benjamin, "The Work of Art in the Age of Mechanical Reproduction"

Achievement in Context

The publication and reception of Benjamin's essay were greatly affected by the political tensions of the period—to the extent that the first version to be published was altered to prevent alienating its intended readership. Most notably, the references to the work of Karl Marx in the opening lines of the early versions of the essay were eliminated by the editors at the Institute for Social Research as they prepared a translation of the unpublished essay to appear in French.[3] References to "fascism" were altered to the less explicit "totalitarian regimes."[4] After much discussion, and due to his desperate financial situation, Benjamin reluctantly accepted the editorial changes. This was partly because he wanted to find an outlet for his thoughts at a time when many former channels of publication had been closed to him by the dictates of the Nazis: publishing with the Institute for Social Research, in other words, was his last chance. The English version that is the primary focus of this analysis is a translation of the third version of the essay in which the reference to Marx and fascism are restored (and which includes a longer discussion of the significance of film for a cultural and political analysis of art and technology).

The editorial softening of Benjamin's revolutionary tone in the essay reflects the Institute's efforts to not alienate their new host country (the Institute moved to New York City in 1934 to avoid Nazi persecution).[5] The changes are also evidence of critical points of disagreement between Benjamin and the Institute's leaders. In particular, Adorno saw Benjamin's contact with Bertolt Brecht as contaminating the originality of the essay's insights with a certain kind of romantic optimism.[6] According to Adorno, Brecht's influence led Benjamin to adopt an overly optimistic idea of a spontaneous revolutionary potential contained in the new technologies of reproduction rather than engaging in a more theoretically systematic analysis.[7] The version the Institute published was thus a compromise between Adorno's more critical view of mass culture and Benjamin's radical optimistic one.

Limitations

It could be argued that Benjamin's focus on specific forms of technologically reproducible works of art—photography and film—and on the historical shifts that instigated or resulted from their development, limits its applicability. In an age where such media as photography and film have become increasingly integrated with other technologies, some of Benjamin's thesis is arguably less important than it was when he first conceived it.

It is likewise necessary to point out that the changes Benjamin envisaged new technologies could bring about have not come to pass. The very "shock" effects that Benjamin identifies in montage, close-ups, and special effects, have become a hallmark of mainstream cinema that the audience expects. Benjamin saw special effects as the equivalent to the shock value that Dada and Surrealism sought to provoke through their experimental art works, which were intended to prevent the kind of contemplation and studied critique that more traditional paintings afford.[8] Dadaists sought to "outrage the public" by making their art works "the center of scandal"[9]—the most famous example of this is Marcel Duchamp's decision to sign and exhibit a urinal. Rather than pleasing the eye, "the work of art of the Dadaists became an instrument of ballistics. It hit the spectator like a bullet, it happened to him."[10] By contrast, just as Surrealism and Dada are now seen as integral parts of art history and exhibited in some of the most famous art museums, the optics Benjamin views to be revolutionary have become commonplace. Similarly, Benjamin's analysis of the aura that withers around the work of art in an age of technological reproducibility seems unable to account for the blockbuster art exhibitions that tour the globe and attract millions of visitors. Such exhibitions successfully market the authenticity of the original work of art as a literally unique selling point.

1. Anca Pusca, ed. Walter Benjamin and the *Aesthetics of Change* (New York and Basingstoke: Palgrave Macmillan, 2010), esp. Konstantinos Vassiliou, "The Aura of Art After the Advent of the Digital", 158–170.

2. Susan Sontag, "The Decay of Cinema", *New York Times* (February 25, 1996), accessed July 13, 2017, http://www.nytimes.com/books/00/03/12/specials/sontag-cinema.html.

3. Esther Leslie, "The Work of Art in the Age of Unbearable Capitulation", in *Walter Benjamin: Overpowering Conformism* (London: Reaktion, 2000), 130–167.

4. Leslie, "The Work of Art in the Age of Unbearable Capitulation", 131.

5. Leslie, "The Work of Art in the Age of Unbearable Capitulation", 130 and 131.

6. Theodor W. Adorno and Walter Benjamin, *The Complete Correspondence: 1928–1940*, trans. Nicholas Walker (Cambridge: Polity, 1999), 127–134 (130).

7. Adorno and Benjamin, *The Complete Correspondence*, 130.

8. Walter Benjamin, "The Work of Art in the Age of Mechanical Reproduction", in *Illuminations*, ed. Hannah Arendt (London: Pimlico, 1999), 231.

9. Benjamin, "The Work of Art", 231.

10. Benjamin, "The Work of Art", 231.

MODULE 8
PLACE IN THE AUTHOR'S WORK

KEY POINTS

* The final version of "The Work of Art in the Age of Mechanical Reproduction" was Benjamin's penultimate work, published a year before his alleged suicide.
* "The Work of Art" builds on previous ideas that Benjamin explored in his essays on photography and literature and the Paris arcades.
* Benjamin's best-known essay has become less central as previously unpublished writing by the author has come to light.

Positioning

Completed in 1939, only a year before his suspected suicide, the third and final version of "The Work of Art" is one of Benjamin's last works. However, the essay's focus on the conditions of the production of art, photography, and film, and on the political ramifications of art, relates to themes present throughout Benjamin's work. In particular, the essay builds on his earlier essay, "A Small History of Photography,"[1] where he explored a shift in the physical act of seeing brought about by photography. In this earlier essay he argued that "the destruction of the aura is the mark of a perception whose sense of the sameness of things has grown to the point where even the singular, the unique, is divested of its uniqueness—by means of its reproduction."[2] He also proposed the concept of the "optical unconscious"[3] that recurs in a slightly different form in "The Work of Art," where he argues that the photographic and cinematic processes of the close-up and slow motion expose "entirely new structural formations of the subject" in a similar way to how psychoanalysts expose unconscious impulses.[4]

Affinities can also be found between "The Work of Art" and "The Author as Producer" (1934), which argues that under capitalism, publishing inherently participates in class conflict.[5] Thus the writer takes sides whether or not they are aware of it. Benjamin calls for the writer to side with the working classes (proletariat), and to combat the fascist tendencies inherent in the capitalist mode of production both through the content of their work and at the level of form. Writers should not see themselves as suppliers of works that fit into existing formal categories, but as *producers* of radical new forms. However, while "The Author as Producer" explores parallel ideas to "The Work of Art" (with regard to printing rather than photography/film), its hardline Marxist approach arguably renders it a less sophisticated or nuanced work.

⌐ *All knowledge takes the form of interpretation*

—— Walter Benjamin, *The Correspondence of Walter Benjamin*, 1910–1940 ⌐

Integration

Benjamin's concern in "The Work of Art" with the material conditions underlying artistic production, in turn aligns it with the themes of the *Arcades Project*, the book he spent the last thirteen years of his life writing.[6] The project focused on the early-nineteenth-century architectural form of Parisian passages (shopping arcades), which Benjamin saw as a symbol of capitalist delusion. Once the center of commerce, by the end of the nineteenth century the arcades had been made obsolete by department stores. Benjamin saw the now empty, derelict spaces of the arcades as symbolizing a culture in which today's prized possession is tomorrow's trash.

"The Work of Art" also bears some relation to "The Storyteller," an essay Benjamin was writing in the same period, which addressed a comparable erosion of the craft of storytelling as a consequence of the reproductive technologies of print.[7]

Finally, "The Work of Art" intersects with Benjamin's other work in its celebration of distraction. Benjamin spent the 1910s translating the work of the French poet Charles Baudelaire who, in "The Painter of Modern Life" (1863),* argued that modern urban life necessitated new modes of representation capable of capturing the constant flux and change of the capitalist city. For Baudelaire, the figure of the *"flâneur"** (French for wanderer) embodies the qualities required of the modern poet: openness to absorbing (and writing about) the many shocks and stimuli of the city. Benjamin argued that in the twentieth century, such an approach was no longer possible: the possibility of *flânerie* was killed off by consumer capitalism. Twentieth-century capitalism's constant requirement of its citizens to take part in the processes of consumption and exchange renders distracted wandering unfeasible. Thus, in "The Work of Art," Benjamin identifies film as a new source for the measured distraction enjoyed by the nineteenth-century *flâneur*: not passive enjoyment, but rather a distanced and dispassionate engagement.[8]

Significance

While the argument of "The Work of Art" is fundamentally unique, Benjamin's unorthodox methodology here is characteristic of his work in general. His thinking consistently involves connecting various fragments from seemingly separate disciplines, such as art, architecture, film, photography, history, literature, philosophy, and politics. By grouping these fragments together within his essay, he constructs an innovative approach to thinking about art and politics, cultural production, and technological reproduction.

As the most widely read work of one of the most influential critics of the twentieth century, "The Work of Art" has proved to be a "game-changer" (albeit belatedly, many years after his death). Since the publication of the first English translation in the late 1960s, the essay has served for many people as a valuable introduction to Benjamin's corpus and remains a key reference point for the study of twentieth-century culture and modernity.

However, in more recent years, the essay has been less central to discussions of Benjamin's continued significance as a critic and theorist. This is largely owing to scholars' increased interest in other essays by Benjamin—most notably, "Theses on the Philosophy of History."[9] Benjamin's last completed work, this essay is a critique of historicism* (the attribution of meaning to historical circumstances, and the analysis of phenomena in relation to their historical context).

The diminishing centrality of "The Work of Art" in contemporary intellectual debate is also a consequence of the emergence in translation of various other material published after Benjamin's death.[10] Most notably, writings the Gestapo confiscated from Benjamin's last apartment in Paris were only transferred to the Walter Benjamin Archive in Berlin in 1996.[11] The two biographies of Benjamin, by Esther Leslie* in 2007 and by Howard Eiland* and Michael W. Thompson in 2013, have also contributed to new directions in Benjamin studies.[12] These writings have inspired a flood of commentary on lesser-researched aspects of Benjamin's work, as well as new translations. Thus, while "The Work of Art" remains important, it has arguably already fulfilled its original task—to open Benjamin's complex output to a seemingly endless process of interpretation.

1. Walter Benjamin, "A Small History of Photography", in *One-Way Street and Other Writings*, trans. Edmund Jephcott, and Kingsley Shorter (London: Verso, 1999), 240–257.

2. Benjamin, "A Small History of Photography", 250.

3. Benjamin, "A Small History of Photography", 243.

4. Walter Benjamin, "The Work of Art in the Age of Mechanical Reproduction", in *Illuminations*, ed. Hannah Arendt (London: Pimlico, 1999), 229.

5. Walter Benjamin, "The Author as Producer", in *Understanding Brecht*, trans. Anna Bostock (London: Verso, 2003), 85–103.

6. Walter Benjamin, *Arcades Project*, ed. and trans. Howard Eiland and Kevin McLaughlin (Cambridge, MA: Belknap/Harvard University Press, 1999).

7. Walter Benjamin, "The Storyteller", in *Illuminations*, trans. Harry Zohn (London: Fontana, 1982), 83–109.

8. Benjamin, "The Work of Art," 233–234.

9. Walter Benjamin, "Theses on the Philosophy of History", in *Illuminations*, trans. by Harry Zohn (London: Fontana, 1982), 255–266. This essay has also been widely translated as "On the Concept of History".

10. Rolf J. Goebel, "Introduction: Benjamin's Actuality", in *A Companion to the Works of Walter Benjamin,* ed. Rolf J. Goebel (London: Camden House, 2009), 2.

11. Goebel, "Introduction: Benjamin's Actuality", 2.

12. Esther Leslie, *Walter Benjamin* (London: Reaktion, 2007); Howard Eiland and Michael W. Jennings, *Walter Benjamin: A Critical Life* (Cambridge, MA: Belknap Press/Harvard University Press, 2013).

SECTION 3
IMPACT

THE FIRST RESPONSES

KEY POINTS

* The initial reception of "The Work of Art in the Age of Mechanical Reproduction" came before publication, from the leaders of the Institute for Social Research.

* Benjamin addressed the leaders' criticisms in a prolonged correspondence with Theodor Adorno.

* While some of the ideas in "The Work of Art" are flawed, the text is important to the study of twentieth-century art, technology, and politics.

Criticism

When "The Work of Art in the Age of Mechanical Reproduction" was first published in 1936 in the journal of the Institute for Social Research (in a French translation), it failed to stimulate the kind of ongoing debate about the relationship between aesthetics and politics that Benjamin had hoped.[1] It would be almost two decades before the essay was republished in Benjamin's native German, and three decades before its first appearance in an English translation, in 1968, that would help to ignite an explosion of interest in Benjamin's work.[2]

The first criticisms of the text came before its actual publication, from the scholars at the Institute of Social Research who had commissioned the piece, and with whom Benjamin was loosely affiliated. Adorno, in particular, engaged in an important discussion with Benjamin about the essay's merits and flaws.[3]

This discussion can be found in Benjamin's correspondence with Adorno, and particularly in a letter Adorno wrote in March 1936.[4] Here Adorno criticized Benjamin's essay for its overly optimistic view of the revolutionary potential of film: "if anything can be said to possess an auratic character now, it is precisely film which does so, and to an extreme and highly suspect degree."[5] Adorno argued that it was "simple romanticization" to think that "a reactionary individual [could] be transformed into a member of the avant-garde"* just by watching a silent movie.[6] He opined that "the laughter of a cinema audience [was] anything but salutary and revolutionary"[7] and remained unconvinced by Benjamin's theory of distraction, "if only for the simple reason that in a communist society, work would be organized in such a way that human beings would no longer be so exhausted or so stupefied as to require distraction."[8]

Adorno also pointed out "how little" use films made of the optical effects Benjamin considered to hold so much radical potential. Most films, he commented, merely attempted to replicate reality.[9] He did, however, agree with Benjamin's assessment of Dada's techniques of shock as anticipating the shock effects of film.[10] Adorno's criticisms should also be understood as stemming from his own bias towards Benjamin's other work—he expressly stated in another letter: "I regard your work on the 'Arcades' as the center not merely of your own philosophy, but as the decisive philosophical word which must find utterance today."[11]

> [Adorno] asks, which art unmasks more effectively the
> barbaric circumstances that we inhabit? Both the highest,
> Kafka and Shoenberg, with their non-auratic, technically
> advanced and barbaric art without pleasure, and the
> lowest, Disney, Chaplin, and the art of the philistines, bear
> the stigmata and elements of change ... Mickey [Mouse's]
> magic magics away the urgency of social transformation.
>
> —— Esther Leslie, *Hollywood Flatlands,*
> *Critical Theory and the Avant-Garde*

Responses

Although Benjamin acknowledged that Adorno's comments and criticisms were instructive, by the time he wrote the third version of the essay he had decided to maintain his position. In fact, he even removed his discussion of the fascist aspects of the violence in Mickey Mouse, which he had inserted into the essay's second version, and which anticipated Adorno's criticisms of Disney in "The Culture Industry."[12] To address Adorno's concerns, however, he supplemented the essay with lengthy footnotes. These footnotes, as leading Benjamin scholar Esther Leslie notes, betray Benjamin's ambivalent views towards cinema as both potentially liberating and potentially oppressive.[13] In Footnote Seven, for example, Benjamin explains how the development of sound film helped overcome the language barrier that was preventing international distribution and that was thus serving the nationalistic interests of fascism (which holds that viewing foreign works of art is unpatriotic). He argues that "viewed from the outside, the sound film promoted national interests, but seen from the inside it helped to internationalize film production even more than previously."[14]

Likewise, as Leslie notes, the epilogue of Benjamin's essay "reverse[s] the optimistic current—all the potential credited to art in the age of technology evaporated before the techno-mysticism and class-violence of the Nationalist Socialists."[15] In her words, Benjamin recognizes in this last section how "fascists mirrored mass society in representations without substance" by representing the masses formally (that is, depicting them on film), without "represent[ing] [them] politically in any meaningful way."[16] In tempering the optimism expressed in the other sections, Benjamin can be seen to address Adorno's concerns.

Conflict and Consensus

Because Benjamin died so soon after the completion of the essay's final draft, these disagreements with Adorno were never fully resolved—and scholars have, in fact, continued to debate them in the decades since. Likewise, while the essay did not generate the immediate response for which he hoped, it has since been recognized as a pioneering contribution to the study of political aesthetics—a discipline that examines the role of beauty and artistic representation in a political context, and which he, Adorno, Horkheimer, and others associated with the Frankfurt School, helped create.

The explosion of interest in Benjamin's essay in an English-language context since the nineteen seventies, after its translation into English in 1968, reflects a wider shift in what scholars deem worth studying. Benjamin's view that mass culture deserves to be examined as much as "High Culture,"* and that such examination should be purely negative in its assessment, anticipated later developments in literary studies and the social sciences. Like Benjamin's work, the field of Cultural Studies, for example, is premised on the idea that all cultural phenomena, not just those produced by and for the upper classes, are worthy of scholarly attention. Thus, while the commercial history of film in the post-World War II era makes Benjamin's revolutionary hopes for film appear naïve, its nuanced analyses make it a seminal artifact of 1930s critical thought, and an important predecessor to later film theory and cultural studies more broadly.[17] While its assessment of technology's long-term impact on art and culture under capitalism is arguably flawed, its attempt to understand these forms in the first place is important.

---

1. Esther Leslie, "Revolutionary potential and Walter Benjamin: A postwar reception history", in *Critical Companion to Contemporary Marxism*, ed. Gregory Elliott and Jacques Bidet (Leiden: Brill, 2007), 549–566.

2. Leslie, "Revolutionary potential and Walter Benjamin", 549–566.

3. Theodor W. Adorno and Walter Benjamin, *The Complete Correspondence: 1928–1940*, trans. Nicholas Walker (Cambridge: Polity, 1999), 127–134.

4. Adorno and Benjamin, *The Complete Correspondence*, 127–134 (130).

5. Adorno and Benjamin, *The Complete Correspondence*, 132.

6. Adorno and Benjamin, *The Complete Correspondence*, 130.

7. Adorno and Benjamin, *The Complete Correspondence*, 130.

8. Adorno and Benjamin, *The Complete Correspondence*, 130.

9. Adorno and Benjamin, *The Complete Correspondence*, 131.

10. Adorno and Benjamin, *The Complete Correspondence*, 133.

11. Adorno and Benjamin, *The Complete Correspondence*, 85.

12. Esther Leslie, *Hollywood Flatlands, Critical Theory and the Avant-Garde* (London: Verso, 2002), 117–118. Benjamin's discussion of Disney can be found in *Walter Benjamin, The Work of Art in the Age of Its Technological Reproducibility and Other Writings on Media*, ed. Michael W. Jennings, Brigid Doherty, Thomas Y. Levin (Cambridge, MA: The Belknap Press, 2008), 318–338.

13. Leslie, *Hollywood Flatlands*, 117–118.

14. Walter Benjamin, "The Work of Art in the Age of Mechanical Reproduction", in *Illuminations*, ed. Hannah Arendt (London: Pimlico, 1999), 237.

15. Esther Leslie, *Walter Benjamin* (London: Reaktion, 2007), 162.

16. Leslie, *Walter Benjamin*, 163.

17. Angela McRobbie, "The *Passagenwerk* and the place of Walter Benjamin in cultural studies", *Cultural Studies* 6. 2 (1992): 147–169. Reprinted in *The Cultural Studies Reader*, ed. Simon During (London: Routledge, 1999), 77–96. See also Andrew Robinson, "Walter Benjamin and Critical Theory", *Ceasefire* (April 4, 2013), accessed July 13, 2017, https://ceasefiremagazine.co.uk/in-theory-benjamin-1/.

THE EVOLVING DEBATE

KEY POINTS

* "The Work of Art in the Age of Mechanical Reproduction" has a complex history as multiple versions of the essay exist, and its translation into English was delayed.
* Benjamin's essay is a pioneering work of political aesthetics and critical theory, and it has influenced art criticism and art history.
* Benjamin scholarship is roughly split between those who apply his ideas to the study of mass culture, and those who read them politically.

Uses and Problems

The story of the production and dissemination of Benjamin's essay is itself convoluted due both to its author's premature death and to the multiple versions and translations of it that exist. Benjamin wrote the original version in German in 1935. He then wrote a second version, which the Institute for Social Research modified, omitting the original's references to Marx, and translated into French before publishing it.[1] The final version, which Benjamin finished in 1939 and in which he re-introduced the previously omitted parts, was published in Germany in 1955 in an essay collection titled *Schriften*.[2]

The first English language edition of *Schriften*, edited by the noted German intellectual Hannah Arendt and translated by Harry Zohn as *Illuminations*, was published in 1968, featuring an introductory essay by Arendt that first appeared in *The*

New Yorker.* This translation followed other appropriations of Benjamin's work by university students in West Germany,* who exchanged pirate copies of his work during the student revolts of the late 1960s.[3] At a time of mass protests against establishment values (exemplified by the Paris uprisings* in May 1968), the Vietnam War,* racism, colonialism,* and social inequality, Benjamin's work gained new resonance.

Interest in "The Work of Art" fueled the translation into English of Benjamin's other work, previously either unpublished or only available in German. A first collection of his correspondence, edited by Adorno and published in Germany in 1978, was translated into English in 1994.[4] This was followed by an English translation of *The Arcades Project* in 1999, and of Adorno and Benjamin's complete correspondence in 2001.[5] Finally, two new translations of "The Work of Art" came out between 2008 and 2009: one, by J.A. Underwood, of the final version of the essay, and another, by Michael Jennings, of the second version, under the title "The Work of Art in the Age of Its Technological Reproducibility."[6] This latter title more accurately reflects the German original and more faithfully conveys Benjamin's wider interest in ideas related to *Technik*, a term that relates to both technique and technology— although Zohn's 1968 version remains the more frequently read.

> Benjamin desires to ... release ... the potential of technology. Technology must be made to work for social transformation rather than enforcing the soporific dream state. The bourgeoisie sustains the dream state by conserving the relations of production in which technology is entwined ...

The proletariat ... possesses the ability to revive collectively,
through a realization of class-consciousness.

—— Esther Leslie, *Walter Benjamin:*
Overpowering Conformism

Schools of Thought

Benjamin's essay has had a wide-ranging influence and it contributed directly to the very foundation of two schools of thought. Together with Max Horkheimer, Theodor Adorno, Erich Fromm* and Herbert Marcuse,* Benjamin helped establish the discipline of critical theory. In his essay "Traditional and Critical Theory" (1937),* Horkheimer states that a theory is critical if it seeks to "liberate human beings from the circumstances that enslave them."[7] In contrast to the "traditional" methods of natural scientists, who merely seek to explain phenomena, critical theory aims to both investigate and challenge the status quo— and particularly capitalism's influence on power structures. As a text that explores technological reproduction in order to forge ways of opposing dominant modes of thinking, Benjamin's essay can be seen as among the very first works of critical theory.

Benjamin and his Frankfurt School colleagues likewise laid the groundwork for political aesthetics. Benjamin's famous statements in the epilogue of "The Work of Art," that "The logical result of Fascism is the introduction of aesthetics into political life" and that "[a]ll efforts to render politics aesthetic culminate in one thing: war,"[8] are among the foundational concepts of political aesthetics, which is likewise concerned with how political ideas and movements expressed and represented in culture serve to advance ideological shifts or to uphold oppressive regimes.

Within art history and criticism, writer and art critic John Berger (1926–2017) famously incorporated ideas from Benjamin's essay into his 1970s television series *Ways of Seeing*.* The show was subsequently adapted as a popular introductory book on art history that is now widely used on university syllabi.[9] In the first chapter of the book of *Ways of Seeing*, Berger explains that the reverence individuals are encouraged to feel towards artworks as unique, unchanging objects is related to broader efforts to keep the dominant class in place. When a work of art becomes technically reproducible another set of assumptions (or what he calls "mystifications") threaten to set in: these need to be challenged. At the end of the chapter he acknowledges his intellectual debt to Benjamin's essay.[10]

In Current Scholarship

Crudely summarized, Benjamin scholarship since the 1970s can be split into two strands. First, there are those within the US strand of cultural studies, which in contrast to its UK counterpart has, since the mid-1980s, tended to examine mass culture apolitically.[11] For many years, US cultural studies tended to approach Benjamin as a critic on the margins of academia—since Benjamin did not hold an academic post—to be praised for his focus on everyday phenomena and his appreciation of film and photography as worthy of attention.[12] Such scholarship largely ignored the political dimensions of Benjamin's work, and is arguably symptomatic of the broader decline in the popularity of critical theory in US academia during the 1980s and 1990s that resulted from the dominance of neoliberal* ideology fueled by the Reagan* and Bush* administrations, and the perceived triumph of capitalism over communism* after the collapse of the Soviet Union* in 1991. In the wake of communism's defeat, and at a time of relative economic prosperity, there appeared to be little need to examine anti-capitalist writing—a view that the US novelist Jonathan Franzen* parodies in his 2001 novel, *The Corrections*, where the English professor protagonist sells off all of his Frankfurt School books (including Benjamin's) for pennies.[13]

These de-politicized applications of Benjamin's work were anticipated by the Marxist literary critic* Terry Eagleton* in his 1981 study, *Walter Benjamin; or, Towards a Revolutionary Criticism* (1981), where he openly stated his aim to "get to Benjamin before the opposition does."[14] The second strand of Benjamin scholarship echoes Eagleton in its efforts to oppose the dilution of Benjamin's radicalism. From the perspective of these scholars, Benjamin's essay is first and foremost the work of an exiled German Jew involved in opposing capitalism, fascism, and war. Only from this basis does it become possible to use the text in ways that illuminate our own cultural, historical, political, and social contexts. Thus, in *Walter Benjamin: Against Conformism* (2000), one of the first books in English to reclaim Benjamin's politics, Esther Leslie argues that Benjamin's work as a whole should be understood as actively engaging with the prospect of a "military atrocity ... intensified by technological means."[15]

1. Esther Leslie, "The Work of Art in the Age of Unbearable Capitulation", in *Walter Benjamin: Overpowering Conformism* (London: Reaktion, 2000), 131.

2. Walter Benjamin, *Schriften* (Frankfurt am Main: Suhrkamp Verlag, 1955).

3. Esther Leslie, *Walter Benjamin* (London: Reaktion, 2007), 227.

4. Walter Benjamin, *Arcades Project,* ed. and trans. Howard Eiland and Kevin McLaughlin (Cambridge, MA: Belknap/Harvard University Press, 1999).

5. Theodor W. Adorno and Walter Benjamin, *The Complete Correspondence: 1928–1940*, trans. Nicholas Walker (Cambridge: Polity, 1999).

6. Walter Benjamin, "The Work of Art in the Age of Mechanical Reproduction", in *One-Way Street and Other Writings,* ed. Amit Chaudhuri and trans. J.A. Underwood (London and New York: Penguin, 2008), 228–259; "The Work of Art in the Age of Its Technological Reproducibility", in *The Work of Art in the Age of Its Technological Reproducibility and Other Writings on Media*, ed. Michael W. Jennings, Brigid Doherty, Thomas Y. Levin (Cambridge, MA: Belknap/Harvard University Press, 2008).

7. Max Horkheimer, "Traditional and Critical Theory" (1937), in *Selected Essays* (London and New York: Continuum, 1982), 188–244 (244).

8. Benjamin, "The Work of Art", 234.

9. John Berger, *Ways of Seeing* (London: Penguin, 1977), 34.

10. Berger, *Ways of Seeing,* 34.

11. John Clarke, "Cultural Studies: A British Inheritance", in *New Times and Old Enemies: Essays on Cultural Studies and America* (New York: Harper Collins, 1991); Robert W. McChesney, "Whatever happened to cultural studies?", in *American Cultural Studies,* ed. Catherine A. Warren and Mary Douglas Vavrus (Chicago: University of Illinois Press, 2002), 76–93; Cary Nelson, "Always Already Cultural Studies", in *English Studies/Cultural Studies: Institutionalizing Dissent,* ed. Isaiah Smithson and Nancy Ruff (Chicago: University of Illinois Press, 1994), 191–206.

12. For an example of this critique, see Janet Wolff, "Memoirs and Micrologies: Walter Benjamin, feminism, and cultural analysis", in *Walter Benjamin: Critical Interventions in Cultural Theory. Vol III: Appropriations*, ed. Peter Osborne (London: Routledge, 2005), 319–333.

13. Jonathan Franzen, *The Corrections* (London: Fourth Estate, 2001), 106.

14. Terry Eagleton, *Walter Benjamin; or, Towards a Revolutionary Criticism* (London: Verso, 1981), ii.

15. Esther Leslie, "The Work of Art in the Age of Unbearable Capitulation", 1.

IMPACT AND INFLUENCE TODAY

KEY POINTS

• "The Work of Art in the Age of Mechanical Reproduction" remains a reference point for scholars interested in twentieth-century art, culture, technology, and politics.

• Benjamin scholars have recently critiqued Benjamin studies' own complicity in downplaying the more radical aspects of Benjamin's work.

• Scholars also debate the ethical implications of the depoliticized portrayal of Benjamin in undergraduate guides to his work.

Position

"The Work of Art in the Age of Mechanical Reproduction" is still considered a pioneering work of scholarship, and it continues to be anthologized, taught in university classrooms, and referenced in academic scholarship. This is partly because the essay anticipated or provided the groundwork for contemporary discussions about the relationship between art, technology, and politics. It is also because Benjamin's ideas help shed light on the work of his artist and writer contemporaries. "The Work of Art" surfaces in countless books on early-twentieth-century art, cinema, photography, and literature. For example, the essays in Pamela Caughie's edited collection, *Virginia Woolf in the Age of Mechanical Reproduction* (2000), apply Benjamin's ideas to highlight the significance of technological reproducibility in the life and fiction of British author Virginia Woolf.[*1] Likewise, Lara Feigel's *Literature, Cinema, and*

Politics 1930–1945: Reading Between the Frames (2010), adopts Benjamin's ideas to examine the relationship between film and literature in the immediate run-up to, and during, World War II.[2]

Beyond these historical studies, Benjamin's essay is cited in discussions concerning digital technology.[3] Rolf Goebel, for example, notes that Benjamin's view of the radical potential of new technologies to disrupt the status quo is vindicated by "virtual reality scenarios that can be received all over the world" and in which "the aura of authenticity and uniqueness—both with respect to works of art and topographic sites—seems increasingly to disappear."[4]

These media have the "salutary" effect of "demystify[ing] the terrifying or intriguing strangeness of faraway lands"—making us more likely to empathize with those different from us, and providing a corrective to authoritarian* rulers' efforts to pit nations against each other.[5] At the same time, digital media have the capacity to endow specific images of political unrest or protest with universal qualities, rendering them emblems of pro-democratic movements globally.[6] "In contrast to Benjamin's identification of political aura with Fascism, this kind of aestheticizing of politics by the mass media is now coded as democratic self-articulation and anti-authoritarian defiance."[7]

> The mere existence of a 'Benjamin industry' is not in itself
> extraordinary. The commodification* of various intellectuals
> is a common capitalist phenomenon, especially in the age
> of mass media and broader access to education, as witness
> by the popularity of James Joyce fridge magnet dolls or

Sigmund Freud slippers.

——Udi E. Greenberg, "The Politics of the Walter
Benjamin Industry"

Interaction

One of the recurring questions debated by Benjamin scholars today regards whether assuming his work to be universally applicable in fact goes against its very ethos, which sought to examine cultural phenomena within their specific historical context. A second relates to whether meaningful Benjamin scholarship is possible at a time when universities themselves are increasingly under pressure to discourage radical thinking. A third regards the need to critically examine the history of Benjamin scholarship *itself*, and to acknowledge that it, too, has been shaped by capitalist ideology— and that there is something questionable about capitalizing (making money) on the ideas of someone so vehemently opposed to capitalist consumer culture.

In a keynote address at the first Congress of the International Walter Benjamin Association in 1997, Benjamin scholar Susan Buck-Morss commented on what she saw to be the "irony" of the very existence of a Walter Benjamin conference, when the writer himself was ostracized by academia for his views.[8] She further argued that meaningful Benjamin scholarship must seek to retain Benjamin's view that "What we do, or do not do, creates the present; what we know, or do not know, constructs the past. These two tasks are inextricably connected in that how we construct the past determines how we understand the present course." Morss's "we" referred to Benjamin scholars themselves, whom she noted have downplayed aspects of "The Work of Art," such as its exploration of Soviet socialist art.

The view that the history of Benjamin scholarship itself requires study is echoed by Esther Leslie in her many articles and books on Benjamin, where she repeatedly calls for more recognition of his radical politics, and, most recently, in *Guardian* journalist Stuart Jeffries's *Grand Hotel Abyss:The Lives of the Frankfurt School* (2016), which traces the evolution of the Institute for Social Research as well as the changing reception and application of its scholars' ideas that has resulted from broader shifts in global politics.[9]

The Continuing Debate

The question about how Benjamin's ideas are used is ultimately an ethical* one. In the broadest terms, ethics are the moral principles that guide our behavior, based on our understanding of what is right and what is wrong. In this case, the question remains whether it is possible to use Benjamin's ideas productively, and in the spirit that he championed, when the very environments in which this occurs (the university classroom, the publishing industry, the conference circuit) are caught up with the capitalist enterprises he opposed. For example, is the ubiquitous presence of Benjamin's work in art museum book stores, or Buzzfeed's* dissemination of Benjamin memes a good thing—helping disseminate his ideas further—or a sign that he has been co-opted?[10]

Scholar Udi E. Greenberg examines these questions in his

2008 essay,"The Politics of the Walter Benjamin Industry," where he traces the assimilation of Benjamin's ideas into popular culture (from experimental musician and artist Laurie Anderson's 1987 film short *What Do You Mean We?* to Benjamin's more recent depiction in the popular 2005 opera *Shadowtime*) before examining academia's own ambiguous relationship to his ideas.[11] According to Greenberg, "Over the last two decades [1988–2008], the German-Jewish thinker was torn from his political context, became a source of personal and ideological identification, and was then returned to the public as a form of socialization."[12] Greenberg goes on to analyze Benjamin's idealized portrayal in publications such as the comic book *Benjamin for Beginners* (2001) and American writer Jay Parini's* novel *Benjamin's Crossing* (1996), to show how "the life and work of the radical thinker were narrated in conservative formulae, producing 'Benjamin' as the signifier not of political subversion, but of social disengagement and disorientation."[13]

---

1. Pamela Caughie, *Virginia Woolf in the Age of Mechanical Reproduction* (London: Routledge, 2000).

2. Lara Feigel, *Literature, Cinema, and Politics 1930–1945: Reading Between the Frames* (Edinburgh University Press, 2010).

3. Freya Schiwy and Alessandro Fornazzari, eds. *Digital Media, Cultural Production and Speculative Capitalism* (London: Routledge, 2013); Jaeho Kang's *Walter Benjamin and the Media: The Spectacle of Modernity* (Cambridge: Polity Press, 2014); Laura J. Shepherd and Caitlin Hamilton, eds. *Understanding Popular Culture and World Politics in the Digital Age* (London: Routledge, 2016).

4. Rolf Goebel, "Introduction: Benjamin's Actuality", in *A Companion to the Works of Walter Benjamin,* ed. Rolf Goebel (London: Camden House, 2009), 1–22.

5. Goebel, 11.

6. Goebel, 11.

7. Goebel, 11.

8. Susan Buck-Morss, "Anti-Stalinist Art: Benjamin, Shostakovich, and the End of the Story", Keynote lecture of the first Congress of the International Walter Benjamin Association, Amsterdam, July 1997. Published as "Revolutionary Time: The Vanguard and the Avant-Garde", in *Benjamin Studies, Studien 1,* ed. Helga Geyer Ryan (Amsterdam: Rodopi, 2002), accessed July 13, 2017, http://susanbuckmorss.info/text/antistalinist-art/.

9. Stuart Jeffries, *Grand Hotel Abyss: The Lives of the Frankfurt School* (London: Verso, 2016).

10. Matt Ortile, "11 Wonderful Illuminating Quotes from Walter Benjamin: Get ready for some *Illuminations* in Honor of His 122nd Birthday Today!", *Buzzfeed* (July 15, 2014), accessed June 30, 2017, https://www.buzzfeed. com/mattortile/work-of-art-in-the-age-of-social-discovery?utm_term=.vb8mqkAAj#.shK5pgyyD.

11. Udi E. Greenberg, "The Politics of the Walter Benjamin Industry," *Theory, Culture & Society* 25, no. 3 (2008): 53–68, accessed June 28, 2017, http://journals.sagepub.com.libproxy.ucl.ac.uk/doi/pdf/10.1177/0263276408090657. DOI: 10.1177/0263276408090657.

12. Greenberg, 61.

13. Greenberg, 68.

WHERE NEXT?

KEY POINTS

* Like its reception to date, future applications of "The Work of Art in the Age of Mechanical Reproduction" will inevitably be shaped by the broader political climate.
* Skepticism of neoliberalism and the rise of the far right in Europe and the US will likely fuel Benjamin scholarship in the near future.
* "The Work of Art" is a key reference for anyone interested in better understanding the relationship between art, technology, and politics.

Potential

The enduring influence of Walter Benjamin's essay across the humanities and social sciences reflects both the essay's originality and acuity and its relevance for understanding the seismic shifts in western—if not global—politics since it was written. What's more, the broader political environment, which has shaped the course of the essay's reception in the near-century since its publication, will also, in all likelihood, affect the direction of Benjamin scholarship in future. Thus, just as the neoliberal political climate of the 1980s and 1990s generated more conservative readings of Benjamin among scholars in English-speaking countries, there are some indications now that the tide has turned towards more radical analyses. For one thing, Benjamin's criticisms of capitalism chime with the questioning of free market ideology (also known as neoliberalism) manifest in much journalism and academic scholarship in the wake of the 2007–2008 global financial crisis,* some of which makes explicit reference to his work.[1] For another, Benjamin's analysis of fascism's manipulation of public opinion has evident applications for understanding the rise of far-right movements in Europe and the US, which has been frequently compared to that of the 1930s.[2]

Finally, Benjamin's work has instigated interest outside of academia since 2015, when Donald Trump first announced his candidacy for the US presidency. A slew of articles during and in the immediate aftermath of the US presidential election cited Benjamin, Adorno, and Horkheimer as key reference points for understanding Trump's theatrics, which they claimed resembled Hitler's deft manipulations of the media.[3]

Each of these events—the global financial crisis and ensuing policy of austerity,* which increased social inequality in much of Europe and the US; the ensuing rise of the far-right, and, in Greece and Spain, the far-left; and the US election—have prompted an unprecedented public interest in Benjamin's ideas.

> *Mass reproduction is aided especially by the reproduction of masses. In big parades and monster rallies, in sports events, and in war, all of which nowadays are captured by camera … the masses are brought face to face with themselves. This process … is intimately connected with the development of the techniques of reproduction and photography.*
>
> ——Walter Benjamin, "The Work of Art in the Age of Mechanical Reproduction"

Future Directions

In light of the political shifts just described, Benjamin's epilogue on war and aesthetics is especially ripe for re-consideration. Here, Benjamin explained how fascism "attempts to organize the newly created proletarian masses without affecting the property structure which the masses strive to eliminate."[4]

Fascism achieves this by creating a cult around its leaders, which then allows it to justify violence and the further production of "ritual values" (values associated with the dictator's regimes, in this case). Not only traditional art forms, but cinema and other forms of mass media can be used for such manipulative purposes. From here, Benjamin argues that only war "makes it possible to mobilize all of today's technical resources while maintaining the property system."[5] Art and technology can help maintain a seemingly unchangeable political position in which the majority of people are kept subordinate to a minority with a vested interest.

While an in-depth application of Benjamin's concept of art, technology, and war to twenty-first century politics remains to be written, scholars and journalists have certainly skirted the edges of the topic through analyses of Trump's use of spectacle to gain and manipulate power.[6] In *The Citizen Marketer: Promoting Political Opinion in the Social Media Age* (2017), for example, Joel Penney applies Benjamin's discussion of the aestheticization of politics to an analysis of Trump's campaign tactics, which included paying people to attend the rally where he announced his candidacy.[7] Mark Andrejevic,* in turn, applies Benjamin's ideas to a discussion of Trump's media persona and the demagoguery* that characterized his campaign.[8] Anthropologists Donna M. Goldstein and Kira Hall have likewise used Walter Benjamin's essay, and the ideas of Benjamin scholar Susan Buck-Morss, to examine Trump's "spectacle of governing."[9]

Beyond these issues, the revolutionary energies that Benjamin's essay identifies are likely to be used to examine the capture and sharing of everyday experience via mobile phones and other audiovisual recording devices. In one aside in his essay, Benjamin already addresses a similar point when registering that with the rise of letters to the editor and other forms of audience engagement at the end of the nineteenth century and the beginning of the twentieth century, "an increasing number of readers became writers."[10]

In fact, in a passage that predates the internet by almost six decades, Benjamin describes a situation very close to at least one geographical section of the contemporary world of online bloggers: "today there is hardly a gainfully employed European who could not, in principle, find an opportunity to publish somewhere or other comments on his work, grievances, documentary reports, or that sort of thing."[11]

Summary

Over the successive decades since its composition, the revolutionary optimism that Benjamin expressed in "The Work of Art in the Age of Mechanical Reproduction" has spectacularly failed to instigate revolutionary change. Film has proved to be a far more reactionary medium than Benjamin had hoped, while for many years scholars approached the essay itself in the exact terms Benjamin sought to oppose, focusing on the changes he identified in art's reception rather than on their political ramifications. From this perspective, one could argue that the essay was co-opted, despite Benjamin's best intentions, not for fascist purposes, but certainly to conservative ends—that is, by critics with no interest in changing the status quo.

Despite these drawbacks, however, "The Work of Art" remains a pivotal text in art history and literary studies, and a touchstone for radical art criticism today. What is more, it effectively laid the groundwork for the fields of cultural studies, media studies, and political aesthetics, enabling the emergence of entirely new ways of examining phenomena as varied as television, celebrity culture, user-generated content,* and memes.* Benjamin's concepts of the withered aura, cult value, and ritual value continue to be used by art historians, while his identification of the aestheticization of politics in the age of radio, film, and photography anticipated subsequent debates around politics in the age of television, social media, and reality shows. For all of these reasons, "The Work of Art" still has much to teach us, both in terms of how we view art and experience new media, and in terms of art and new media's capacity to change our worldview—for better or for worse.

1. Roger Berkowitz and Taun N. Toay, eds. *The Intellectual Origins of the Global Financial Crisis* (New York: Fordham University Press, 2013), 164–165; Philip Mirowski, *Never Let a Serious Crisis Go to Waste: How Neoliberalism Survived the Financial Meltdown* (London: Verso, 2013), 84, 100. Miriam Meissner, *Narrating the Global Financial Crisis: Urban Imaginaries and the Politics of Myth* (New York and Basingstoke: Palgrave, 2017), 21; 40–45.

2. For a sense of these discussions, see: John Palmer, "The rise of the far right parties across Europe is a chilling echo of the 1930s", *Guardian* (November 15, 2013), accessed June 30, 2017, https://www.theguardian.com/commentisfree/2013/nov/15/far-right-threat-europe-integration. Peter Foster, "The rise of the far-right in Europe is not a false alarm", *Telegraph* (May 19, 2016), accessed June 30, 2017, http://www.telegraph.co.uk/news/2016/05/19/the-rise-of-the-far-right-in-europe-is-not-a-false-alarm/. Mark Mardell, "Fascism, the 1930s, and the 21st century", *BBC News* (December 20, 2016), accessed June 30, 2017, http://www.bbc.co.uk/news/uk-politics-38317787. "No, this isn't the 1930s—but yes, this is fascism" *Faculty of History, University of Oxford* (November 16, 2016), accessed June 30, 2017, http://www.history.ox.ac.uk/article/no-isnt-1930s-yes-fascism.

3. Alexander Binnet, "Donald Trump and the Aesthetics of Fascism: What a 20th-century Marxist art critic can teach us about a very 21st-century candidate", *In These Times* (January 28, 2016), accessed June 28, 2017, http://inthesetimes.com/article/18807/donald-trump-and-the-aesthetics-of-fascism. Thomas Dumm, "Degraded fascism, nihilism, and Donald Trump", *Contemporary Condition* (September 2015), accessed June 28, 2017, http://contemporarycondition.blogspot.co.uk/2015/09/degraded-fascism-nihilism-and-donald.html. Alex Ross, "The Frankfurt School Knew Trump Was Coming", *New Yorker* (December 5, 2016), accessed June 28, 2017, http://www.newyorker.com/culture/cultural-comment/the-frankfurt-school-knew-trump-was-coming.

4. Walter Benjamin, "The Work of Art in the Age of Mechanical Reproduction", in *Illuminations,* ed. Hannah Arendt (London: Pimlico, 1999), 234.

5. Benjamin, "The Work of Art", 234.

6. See, for example David Denby, "The Plot Against America: Trump's Rhetoric", *New Yorker* (December 15, 2015), accessed June 30, 2017, http://www.newyorker.com/culture/cultural-comment/plot-america-donald-trumps-rhetoric. Oliver Jones, *Donald Trump: The Rhetoric* (London: Eyewear Publishing, 2016). Ronald Brownstein, "Trump's rhetoric of white nostalgia", *The Atlantic* (June 2, 2016), accessed June 30, 2017, "https:// www.theatlantic.com/politics/archive/2016/06/trumps-rhetoric-of-white-nostalgia/485192/. Sam Leith, "Trump's rhetoric: a triumph of inarticulacy", *Guardian* (January 13, 2017), accessed June 30, 2017, https://www. theguardian.com/us-news/2017/jan/13/donald-trumps-rhetoric-how-being- inarticulate-is-seen-as-authentic.

7. Joel Penney, *Citizen Marketer: Promoting Political Opinion in the Social Media Age* (Oxford: Oxford University Press, 2017), 113.

8. Mark Andrejevic, "The *Jouissance* of Trump", *Television and New Media* 17, no. 7 (2016): 651–655.

9. Donna M. Goldstein and Kira Hall, "Postelection surrealism and nostalgic racism in the hands of Donald Trump", *HAU: Journal of Ethnographic Theory* 7, no. 1 (2017): http://dx.doi.org/10.14318/hau7.1.026.

10. Benjamin, "The Work of Art", 225.

11. Benjamin, "The Work of Art", 225.

➤ GLOSSARY OF TERMS ➤

1. **Aestheticization of politics:** an expression coined by Benjamin (with the help of Bertolt Brecht) to refer to fascist leaders' use of spectacular displays to inspire allegiance to the state and draw attention away from the oppressive realities of their policies.This concept is central to Benjamin's argument in "The Work of Art."

2. **Anti-Semitism:** prejudice, hostility, or discrimination towards Jewish people, which can range from the belief in entrenched stereotypes (e.g. "all Jewish people are tight with money") and use of prejudicial expressions (e.g."to Jew someone down" in reference to haggling for a lower price) to the committing of acts of violence and implementation of discriminatory laws.

3. *Arcades Project* (1927–): Benjamin's last, and unfinished, project, which examined the Paris arcades as symbols of nineteenth-century capitalist modernity.

4. **Art criticism:** the critique of art works, whether in an academic context or in the public arena (for example, for newspapers or magazines). Benjamin's essay is both a work of art criticism and a criticism of traditional art criticism.

5. **"Art for Art's Sake":** a mode of viewing art that emerged in France in the nineteenth century, according to which art works have an inherent, unchanging value that is entirely separate to their moral function or practical use. Benjamin's essay is a critique of this approach and argues that it can all too easily be co-opted for fascist purposes.

6. **Art history:** the academic study of the history and development of visual art works including painting and sculpture. Benjamin's essay seeks to trace an alternative art history that takes into account the material conditions of art production.

7. **Aura:** an elusive term Benjamin coins in "The Work of Art" to denote the originality of a work of art, its separation from and superiority to everyday life, and its capacity to induce reverence in its viewers. The aura is connected to the artwork's cult value and ritualistic role—that is, its historical centrality to rituals related to the church, the monarchy, or ancient rites.

8. **Austerity:** in economics, the conditions created by government cuts to expenditure on public services (e.g. welfare, public housing, health services).

9. **"The Author as Producer":** an essay by Walter Benjamin that outlines ideas he later expanded upon in "The Work of Art." In particular, he argues that there can be no such thing as autonomous or apolitical art. The essay is much more orthodox in its Marxist stance than "The Work of Art" or his later work.

10. **Authoritarianism:** a form of government requiring obedience to authority at the expense of personal liberties. Fascism is a violent, nationalist form of authoritarianism. References to fascism were changed to "authoritarianism" in the first version of Benjamin's essay.

11. **Autonomous/autonomy:** independent/independence; a term Benjamin uses to refer to the art for art's sake movement's insistence on art's independence/ separation from everyday affairs.

12. **Avant-garde (see European Avant-garde)**

13. **Buzzfeed:** a US digital media company based in New York City that specializes in social news and entertainment, with a particular focus on digital media and technology.

14. **Capitalism:** an economic system in which individuals and groups who privately own goods and services control industry and trade, rather than the state. The forum in which trade takes place is the marketplace.

15. **Capitalistic mode of production:** a system involving private (rather than state) ownership of the means of production, which allows the owners of the means of production (*bourgeoisie*) to accumulate wealth by extracting the surplus value (profit margin) of what their employees (*proletariat*) make/sell.

16. *Charles Baudelaire, Tableaux Parisiens* **(1923):** Walter Benjamin's German translation of French poet Charles Baudelaire's (1821–1867) poetry collection, *Tableaux Parisiens*. Baudelaire had a profound influence on Benjamin and re-appears in many of his essays, and in his unfinished work, *The Arcades Project* (1927–).

17. **Cold War (1947–1991):** a period of intense military and political tension following World War II between Western powers (the United States and its NATO allies) and Eastern powers including the Soviet Union, East Germany and China. It formally ended in 1991 with the collapse of the Soviet Union.

18. **Colonialism:** refers to the rule of one country by another, involving unequal power relations between the ruler (colonist) and ruled (colony), and the exploitation of the colony's resources to strengthen the economy of the colonizers' home country.

19. **Collage:** a work of visual art composed of fragments of mixed media (newspaper clippings, magazine cut-outs, etc.) that often do not appear related. Collage emerged as an artistic form in the early twentieth century; its first practitioners sought to blur the boundary between art and everyday life and to challenge capitalism.

20. **Commodification:** the transformation of something into a commodity (something that can be sold or profited from). Benjamin's work examines how commodities can be stripped of their money-making status and used to resist capitalism.

21. **Commodity fetishism:** the transformation of social relations under capitalism into transactions. According to Marx, capitalism transforms social relations between human beings into economic relations between objects. Benjamin was interested in how objects could be stripped of their money-making status and used for radical purposes.

22. **Communism:** an economic system originally proposed by Karl Marx, in which the means of production (e.g. natural resources, factories, manufacturing equipment) are collectively owned. Marx envisioned a communist society as having no social classes. Benjamin's essay proposes a theory of art based on communist ideals to counter fascism's aestheticization of politics.

23. **"The Conquest of Ubiquity" (1928):** essay by French writer Paul Valéry (1871–1945) about the effects of technology on everyday life, in which he also speculates about future technological developments. Benjamin quotes Valéry in his own essay.

24. **Co-option:** the appropriation or assimilation of ideas or work of a smaller, usually weaker, group or individual. Benjamin's essay seeks to formulate a theory of art that will not be co-opted for fascist purposes.

25. **Critical theory:** a discipline founded by Benjamin and his fellow Frankfurt

School scholars in the 1930s, and which aimed to go beyond the remit of "traditional theory" of explaining phenomena to actively find ways of rectifying social ills, such as class inequality and the abuse of power.

26. **Cultural studies:** an academic field of study characterized by a multidisciplinary approach (derived from the social sciences and the humanities) to the study of contemporary (especially mass) culture (Oxford English Dictionary).

27. **"The Culture Industry":** an essay by Max Horkheimer and Theodor Adorno that argues that mass culture under capitalism is an industry whose aim is to keep the masses pacified and accepting of the status quo.

28. **Dada:** a literary and artistic movement at the beginning of the twentieth century that broke with convention in order to create works designed to startle, shock, and scandalize the public. The movement was partly a response to the horrors of World War I, and partly an effort to challenge the commercialization of art and the encroachment of capitalism on all aspects of everyday life—all of which greatly influenced Walter Benjamin.

29. **Demagoguery:** a manipulative form of persuasion based on appealing to people's feelings, prejudices, and base instincts rather than convincing them through logic. The form is usually associated with political dictators and dishonest politicians.

30. **Depoliticize/depoliticization:** the removal of politics from an activity or cultural phenomenon; for example, a depoliticized analysis of a text ignores its political dimensions including any political references within the text itself, focusing on other elements.

31. **Distraction:** that which prevents one from concentrating on something else; the state of being unable to concentrate. Frankfurt School scholars were interested in the distracting effect of mass culture under capitalism; Benjamin argued that it was potentially a good thing.

32. **Ethics:** the moral principles (distinction between what is right and what is wrong) that guide our behavior; the study of how such moral principles are established or followed.

33. **European avant-garde:** generally refers to radical or countercultural European art and literature produced between 1910 and World War II, including

movements such as Cubism, Dada, Surrealism, and Futurism. These movements all shared a concern with breaking with traditional conventions in art.

34. **Fascism:** any right-wing authoritarian regime; Walter Benjamin was concerned specifically with its organization and evolution in Europe during his lifetime, and the degree to which it relied on propaganda, the aestheticization of military power (making military power "beautiful"), and nostalgic motifs (making people long for the past).

35. ***Flâneur:*** a direct translation of the French term for wandering, the word was first used by Charles Baudelaire to define the experience of urban walking in modernity. Benjamin appropriated it in his readings of the nineteenth-century city, arguing that with the supplanting of the Paris arcades with department stores, and the introduction of the standard working day, the potential for true *flânerie* also died.

36. **Frankfurt School:** a term used to refer to several important leftist philosophers and theorists—prolific and influential scholars based at the University of Frankfurt am Main during the 1920s and 1930s, such as the German philosophers Max Horkheimer (1895–1973) and Theodore W.Adorno (1903–1969), who were colleagues of Walter Benjamin.

37. **Futurism:** an experimental art movement that emerged in Italy at the beginning of the twentieth century, and which championed speed, technology, and war, which its leaders said would allow Italy to become a leading European power. The movement was closely associated with Benito Mussolini's fascist party.

38. **Genre:** from the French word for "type," this is a term used to denote the category of an artwork, e.g."mystery," "comedy," "tragedy," "romance," "western," etc. Critics often examine artworks in relation to other works from the same genre, and consider whether an artwork follows or challenges the conventions of its genre.

39. **Gestapo:** Nazi Germany and occupied Europe's official secret police (the word is an abbreviation of *Geheime Staatspolizei*, the German for "Secret State Police." The Gestapo was formed in 1933 and dissolved in May 1945, with Germany's surrender.

40. **Global financial crisis of 2007–2008:** a financial crisis that started in the United States and spread through much of Europe, and that experts have termed the worst economic upheaval since the depression of the 1930s. Because it was instigated by crises in the subprime mortgage market (involving the sale of loans to people who will have trouble repaying them) and in the banking sector, both of which were caused by lax regulations, one effect of has been a renewed criticism of free market capitalism.

41. **Great Depression:** an economic downturn that affected the US and Europe that began with a stock-market crash in 1929, continued for much of the 1930s, and did not officially end until after World War II. The success of the nationalist and xenophobic strands of fascism during this period have been attributed to the dire poverty experienced by people at this time, which created a heightened receptiveness to blaming minorities and Jews for wider systemic problems.

42. **High culture:** a term used to denote works of art produced for and often by the elite, and considered exclusive, rare, and superior to mass culture, which by definition is intended for large audiences.

43. **Historicism:** broadly speaking, the theory that social events and phenomena are determined by history. Benjamin was critical of this view, arguing that any meaningful understanding of past events must take into consideration the material (socio-economic) conditions that caused them.

44. **Institute for Social Research:** together with the University of Frankfurt am Main, this was the center of German intellectual thought in the first half of the twentieth century. From 1930, under the directorship of Max Horkheimer (1895–1973), it was heavily involved in research combining Marxist philosophy and Freudian psychoanalysis. Those associated with the Institute are also known as the "Frankfurt School."

45. **Jewish mysticism:** the academic study of different forms of mysticism throughout Jewish history. Scholars generally attribute the origins of the discipline to the writings of Walter Benjamin's friend and colleague Gershom Scholem (1897–1982), starting with Scholem's *Major Trends in Jewish Mysticism* (1941).

46. *Late Roman Art Industry* **(1905):** a book by art historian Alois Riegl (1858–1905), that sought to understand the art of the Late Roman period by studying both grandiose monuments and everyday objects like belt buckles. This approach, which involved the assumption that objects do not have to be valuable to be worth studying, was a key inspiration for Walter Benjamin.

47. **Literary studies:** the study, interpretation, and evaluation of literary works, including the assessment of their formal characteristics, their reflection or questioning of cultural norms, and/or their socio-political and historical influence.

48. **Marxism (see Western Marxism)**

49. **Marxist literary criticism:** the application of Marxist ideas to the analysis of literary texts, generally involving an emphasis on the economic conditions that produced the text, which the text reflects in its depiction of socio-economic relations.

50. **Mass culture:** a term used to describe the values and ideas that arise from a common/collective exposure to the same media (be these news sources, art, music, or literature). The term "mass" refers to the idea that the culture is being generated by the masses themselves rather than being imposed on them from above—an idea that Benjamin explores in his essay.

51. **Meme:** in the broadest terms, an idea, belief or expression that spreads rapidly throughout culture. More commonly, the term is used in reference to (usually humorous) online images, videos and pieces of text that are copied, modified, and disseminated across the Internet.

52. **Montage:** the literary and cinematic counterpart of collage;* a composite whole made of fragments, images, text, or other media. In film, it refers to the splicing, alteration, or editing of images. In literature, it refers to the splicing of unrelated texts.

53. **Nationalism:** the belief that one's nation is superior to others and that allegiance to the nation should come above all other concerns; an extreme form of patriotism. Nationalism was a central component of the fascist movements that rose to power during Benjamin's time.

54. **National Socialist German Workers' Party:** also known as the Nazi party; the far-right political party that existed in Germany between 1920 and 1945, and rose to power in the 1930s under Adolf Hitler. The party was created to draw workers away from communism, and initially campaigned on an anti-capitalist, anti-bourgeois (middle class), and nationalist platform, but under Hitler the focus shifted to anti-Semitism and anti-Marxism.

55. **Neoliberalism:** also known as free market capitalism, this is a form of capitalism involving little state intervention. Neoliberalism assumes that markets can regulate themselves, and that individuals or companies operating within them require minimal rules or oversight.

56. *The New Yorker*: a US magazine of essays, satire, fiction, commentary, comics, and poetry established in 1925 and published today by Condé Nast. *The New Yorker* is considered something of an institution: Hannah Arendt's 1968 essay on Walter Benjamin in the magazine would have thus made him a household name in intellectual circles.

57. **"The Painter of Modern Life" (1863):** a famous essay by the French poet Charles Baudelaire, in which he calls for artists to change their techniques in order to more fully convey the modern urban experience. Benjamin used the essay in his own writings on nineteenth-century Paris.

58. **Paris shopping arcades:** a series of glass-covered streets erected in the center of Paris at the beginning of the nineteenth century to cater to the new middle classes. They were rendered obsolete by advent of department stores in the latter half of the nineteenth century.

59. **Paris Uprisings of May 1968:** also known as May '68, these events began as a series of student strikes in the city's high schools and university, and were the culmination of several months of student protest against the endemic elitism in the country's education system.

60. **Political aesthetics:** the study of the relationship between art and politics—how political ideas are expressed in art, as well as how political movements adopt artistic strategies, or enlist artists, to promote their particular ideology. "The Work of Art" is an example of political aesthetics, which Benjamin himself helped pioneer.

61. **Psychoanalysis:** a system of thought that seeks to treat mental disorders by examining the relationship between conscious behavior and unconscious thoughts, impulses, and desires. Psychoanalysis had an enormous influence on many of the art and literary movements of Benjamin's day, particularly surrealism. Benjamin himself applies its ideas in his writings on modern art, literature, and nineteenth-century Paris.

62. **Radical:** departing from tradition; breaking with the past; seeking to change the status quo; fundamentally altering something. Benjamin's work espouses radical views, and he is interested in how reproducibility might aid in opposing fascism and radically changing society.

63. **Reactionary:** right-wing, conservative, or otherwise opposed to social reform or progress. Benjamin's work seeks to combat fascism's reactionary tendencies, which involved the celebration of a largely mythical past, and to instead mobilize cinema and photography to effect positive social change.

64. **Reichstag:** a historic building in Berlin (Germany), opened in 1894 and home to the Imperial Diet (parliament) of the German Empire until 1933 when the fascist party set it on fire.

65. **Rhetoric:** the art of persuasive speech or writing, which involves exploiting figures of speech and particular images that will resonate with the public. Benjamin was interested in the rhetoric used by the fascist part in the late 1930s to mobilize public opinion, which he argued adopted many of the ideas used in traditional art criticism. Rhetoric is also part of what Benjamin sees as the aestheticization of politics in the modern era.

66. **Socialism:** an economic model that involves the communal ownership of the means of production, distribution, and exchange. Within Marxist theory, socialism is a transitional state between the overthrowing of capitalism and the ideal, which is communism.

67. **Soviet Union:** A single-party Marxist-Leninist state comprising fifteen socialist republics in Eastern Europe that existed between 1922 and 1991.

68. **Standstill:** a term used by the playwright Bertolt Brecht to denote a specific moment during a theatrical performance when the action stops, thus jolting

the audience into remembering that this is a performance, as well as allowing them time to critique what is happening. Benjamin wrote extensively about this concept, which also informs his ideas about spectatorship in the age of mechanical reproduction.

69. **Surrealism**: a countercultural artistic movement born in early-twentieth-century Paris as a reaction to consumer culture and to the commercialization of art. The movement sought to challenge boundaries between reality and unreality, the external world and the unconscious mind, and even life and art. These ideas were influenced by Romanticism.

70. **Technique:** in the arts, this refers to the manner in which an artwork (painting, novel, sculpture, etc.) is executed, e.g. broad brushstrokes, or long sentences, or rough edges. This contrasts with the *content*, which instead refers to what the artwork actually communicates.

71. **Technological reproduction:** the copying of an artwork through technological means (e.g. photography), rather than manual replication (e.g. replicating a painting by painting another one).

72. **"Theses on the Philosophy of History" (1940):** a famous essay by Benjamin that critiques historicism and the view of the past as a "a chain of events" marking progress.

73. **Thesis:** a statement put forward in an essay, speech, or other written/ verbal work that the work then seeks to demonstrate. In Benjamin's work, the thesis is part of a "dialectical" approach, which seeks to get at the truth by working out the differences between two opposing views.

74. **Totalitarianism:** a centralized system of government that requires citizens to be completely subservient to the state. While authoritarianism involves the monopoly of power by an individual or small group, totalitarianism involves the individual/ group's efforts to control *all* aspects of social life, and to use the population itself to attain its aims.

75. **"Traditional and Critical Theory" (1937):** an essay by Frankfurt School leader Max Horkheimer that pits the theoretical approach usually found in the natural sciences (involving observation and explanation) against what he calls "critical

theory," which instead seeks to challenge the status quo, and in particular the capitalist order. Walter Benjamin's work can be seen to follow this latter approach.

76. **Urbanization:** refers to the development of rural areas into cities as well as the transformative effects of the growth and expansion of cities. Much of Benjamin's work examines the experience of city living under capitalism, and how the city of Paris in particular functioned as the symbolic center of European capitalism during the nineteenth century.

77. **User-generated content:** a term used to refer to media content authored by the audiences or "users" of a media platform or publication rather than by professional writers. The term is usually used in reference to online media— particularly social media—but also applies to earlier forms, such as the "letter to the editor" format that emerged in newspapers and magazines around 1900.

78. **Vietnam War (1955–1975):** a Cold War-era* conflict fought in Laos, Cambodia, and Vietnam from 1955 to 1975 between the communist regime of North Vietnam and the capitalist South Vietnam. European and US protests against the war from the mid-1960s until its end fed into a broader anti-establishment mood involving the questioning of tradition and authority. It was in this context that the first English-language edition of Benjamin's text appeared.

79. ***Ways of Seeing*:** a 1972 BBC television series hosted by cultural critic John Berger and adapted by Berger in 1973 into a book of the same name. Both the series and the book were designed to criticize traditional art history and drew heavily on Walter Benjamin's essay to do so.

80. **West Germany:** also known as the Federal Republic of Germany (FRG) was the part of Germany that was aligned with other capitalist countries during the Cold War,* from its creation on May 23, 1949 to the fall of the Berlin Wall on October 3, 1990. The Berlin Wall separated West Germany from communist East Germany. The wall divided Berlin itself, so that part of the city belonged to West Germany and the other part to East Germany.

81. **Western Marxism:** a philosophy followed in Western and Central Europe by theorists who apply Marx's ideas, and who are distinct from Marxist philosophers

working within the Soviet Union. The term itself was coined in the 1950s by the French philosopher Maurice Merleau-Ponty, and has been retroactively applied to define the work of Benjamin and others associated with the Frankfurt School.

82. **World War I (1914–1918):** a global war fought between the Allies (led by Russia, France, Italy, the United States, and the UK), and the Central Powers (led by Germany and Austria-Hungary). Germany lost the war and its economy was subsequently ravaged, leading to mass poverty that then paved the way for the rise of fascism.

83. **World War II (1939–1945):** a global war fought between the Allies (led by the Soviet Union, the UK, and the US) and the Axis Powers (led by Germany, Italy, and Japan), which resulted in the genocide of several million Jews across Europe.

PEOPLE MENTIONED IN THE TEXT

1. **Theodor W. Adorno (1903–1969)** was a seminal German philosopher, sociologist and Marxist critic best known for co-authoring *Dialectic of Enlightenment: Philosophical Fragments* with Max Horkheimer. He was a leader of the Institute for Social Research in Frankfurt and a friend of Walter Benjamin.

2. **Hannah Arendt (1906–1975)** was a Jewish German-American writer and political theorist best known for her writings on Nazism, totalitarianism, and violence. She was the editor of the first English translation of *Schriften* (the collection of essays by Benjamin in which "The Work of Art in the Age of Mechanical Reproduction" was first published).

3. **Eugène Atget (1857–1927)** was a French pioneer of documentary photography best known for his efforts to photograph the streets and architecture of Paris before they were demolished, redeveloped, or modernized. Benjamin cites these photographs as evidence of the political nature of modern art.

4. **Georges Bataille (1897–1962)** was a French writer and intellectual involved in the French avant-garde, and a librarian at the central library in Paris when Hitler rose to power. Walter Benjamin left his manuscripts with Bataille when he fled France.

5. **Charles Baudelaire (1821–1867)** was a French essayist, poet and art critic best known for his writings about modernity and the city. His work profoundly influenced Walter Benjamin, who wrote several essays on him as well as translating his poetry.

6. **John Berger (1926–2017)** was an English writer, artist, critic, and political activist. He was the author of many books of art criticism as well as novels, poetry, and documentary essays, of which his most famous, *Ways of Seeing*, is based on "The Work of Art."

7. **Bertolt Brecht (1898–1956)** was a German Marxist playwright, poet, and theatre director, and a close friend of Walter Benjamin's. He is best known for his radical approach to narrative, which is often discussed in relation to the European avant-garde, and his explicit criticisms of capitalism, middle class values, and Nazi Germany.

8. **Susan Buck-Morss** is an American cultural historian and philosopher, and

a leading Walter Benjamin scholar best known for *The Origin of Negative Dialectics:Theodor W.Adorno,Walter Benjamin, and the Frankfurt Institute* (1977) and *The Dialectics of Seeing.Walter Benjamin and the Arcades Project* (1989). She is an ardent critic of the de-politicization of Benjamin's work by art and literature scholars in the US.

9. **George Bush (b. 1924)** is a US Republican politician and served as the 41st president of the USA from 1989 to 1993.

10. **Terry Eagleton (b. 1943)** is a British Marxist literary critic and Distinguished Professor at Lancaster University who studied under the Marxist literary critic Raymond Williams and is best known for his writings on literary theory and Marxist literary studies. Eagleton published a book on Benjamin in 1981 that emphasized his radicalism.

11. **Howard Eiland** is a professor of literature at Harvard University, and a leading translator and editor of several volumes of Walter Benjamin's work, including the first English language edition of the *Arcades Project*. Eiland has also co-written a biography of Benjamin, titled *Walter Benjamin: A Critical Life*.

12. **Friedrich Engels (1820–1895)** was a German philosopher and close colleague of Karl Marx (1818–1883), best known for co-authoring the *Communist Manifesto* (1848). Engels and Marx's work greatly influenced Benjamin.

13. **Jonathan Franzen (b. 1959)** is an American novelist best known for his award-winning novel, *The Corrections* (2001).The protagonist's sale of all of his critical theory books, including Walter Benjamin's, in order to fund an expensive romantic date, has been interpreted as parodying the unpopularity of critical theory in the US during the 1990s, a decade of unusual prosperity.

14. **Erich Fromm (1900–1980)** was a German philosopher, psychologist, and sociologist associated with the Frankfurt School. He is best known for his first book, *Escape from Freedom* (1941), which is considered to be the first work of political psychology, and his later book, *The Art of Loving* (1956).

15. **Adolf Hitler (1889–1945)** was the Führer (leader) of Germany from 1934 to 1945 and was responsible for the persecution and genocide of several million Jews. Benjamin was forced to live in exile in March 1933 due to the Nazis'

requisition of German citizenship from German Jews, and allegedly committed suicide while attempting to escape from occupied France into Spain.

16. **Max Horkheimer (1895–1973)** was a seminal leftist German Jewish sociologist and philosopher and a leader of the "Frankfurt School" best known for his collaborative authorship, with Theodor Adorno, of *Dialectic of Enlightenment: Philosophical Fragments* (1947). Together with Adorno, Horkheimer also published the first version of Benjamin's essay, and funded some of his other research.

17. **Siegfried Kracauer (1889–1966)** was a German Jewish cultural critic, sociologist, film theorist and journalist best known for the essays collected in *The Mass Ornament* (1963). He was a friend of Benjamin's, but disagreed with Benjamin's positive assessment of mass culture, arguing that its distracting qualities served to prevent the masses from revolting.

18. **Esther Leslie (b. 1964)** is a leading scholar of Walter Benjamin's work, and a professor of political aesthetics at Birkbeck College, University of London. Leslie has published a number of books on Benjamin that focus on the political dimension of his writings, and is part of a broader effort to re-politicize his work.

19. **Georg Lukács (1885–1971)** was a Hungarian philosopher and literary critic who later renounced his early work in the alternative Western Marxist tradition that he partly inaugurated with his seminal text *History and Class Consciousness: Studies in Marxist Dialectics*.

20. **Herbert Marcuse (1898–1979)** was a Jewish German-American philosopher and Marxist theorist closely associated with the Frankfurt School and known for his involvement in the student movements of the 1960s in France, Germany, and the US. He escaped the Nazis in 1933 and gained US citizenship in 1940.

21. **Karl Marx (1818–1883)** was a German political philosopher and economist whose analysis of class relations under capitalism and articulation of a more egalitarian system provided the basis for communism. He wrote *The Communist Manifesto* (1848) with Friedrich Engels* (1820–1895); he articulated his full theory of production and class relations in *Das Kapital* (1867–1894).

22. **Maurice Merleau-Ponty (1908–1961)** was a French phenomenological

philosopher and writer, and the only major philosopher of his time to incorporate descriptive psychology in his work. Ponty was strongly influenced by Marxist thought, and is said to have coined the term "Western Marxism."

23. **Jay Parini (b. 1948)** is an American academic and writer best known for his works of criticism, poetry, and biographical novels. In 1997, Parini published a biographical novel about Walter Benjamin's escape from France in 1940, titled *Benjamin's Crossing.*

24. **Dora Sophie Pollak (1890–1964)** was Walter Benjamin's wife between 1918 and 1928, with whom he had a troubled marriage marked by financial insecurity and long periods of separation resulting from Benjamin's writing commitments abroad. The couple had one son, Stefan.

25. **Alois Riegl (1858–1905)** was an Austrian art historian and theorist who was a key figure in the emergence of art history as a distinctive discipline, and is best known for *Problems of Style* (1893) and *Late Roman Art Industry* (1905). Benjamin was influenced by Riegl's view that artworks should be understood in relation to the economic context in which they were produced.

26. **Ronald Reagan (1911–2004)** was a US film actor turned Republican politician who served as the 40th president of the USA from 1981 to 1989.

27. **Gershom Scholem (1897–1982)** was a German-born Israeli historian, philosopher and Jewish mystic, regarded today as one of the founders of the academic study of Kabbalah.

28. **Susan Sontag (1933–2004)** was a Jewish American writer and political activist best known for her books, *On Photography* (1977), *Illness as Metaphor* (1978), and *AIDS and Its Metaphors* (1988), and collections of essays, such as *Under the Sign of Saturn* (1980), which took its title from Sontag's essay on Walter Benjamin, based on an expression he used to describe himself.

29. **Donald Trump (b. 1946)** is a real estate mogul, television celebrity, and the 45th president of the US as of January 2017. Both his deft use of the media during his presidential campaign and his nationalist rhetoric have been repeatedly likened to those of the fascist leaders of the 1930s.

30. **Paul Valéry (1871–1945)** was a French poet and essayist best known for his

involvement with the French symbolist movement in poetry. Walter Benjamin quotes his essay on technology, "The Conquest of Ubiquity" (1928) in "The Work of Art."

31. **Virginia Woolf (1882–1941)** is considered to be among the most influential and important writers of the twentieth century. Woolf is best known for her novel *Mrs Dalloway* (1925) and her essay "A Room of One's Own" (1929). Because of Woolf's extensive engagement with technology in her writing, literary scholars often use Benjamin's ideas in their analyses of her work.

32. **Gustav Wyneken (1875–1964)** was a German educational reformer known for his influential, if controversial, views. His idea that youth groups should be led by older members rather than by adults influenced the German Youth Movement (youth groups focused on outdoor activities). His justification of erotic love between teachers and pupils, however, resulted in his conviction, in 1921, for committing vice with minors. Walter Benjamin attended Wyneken's boarding school between 1905 and 1907 and was highly influenced by his political ideas.

WORKS CITED

1. Adorno, Theodor W. "A Portrait of Walter Benjamin." *Prisms*. Translated by Samuel and Shierry Weber. Cambridge, MA: MIT, 1988. 227–242 (239).

2. — "The Essay as Form." In *Notes to Literature: Volume One*. Translated by Shierry Weber Nicholsen. New York: Columbia University Press, 1991. 3–23 (13).

3. Adorno, Theodor W., and Walter Benjamin. *The Complete Correspondence: 1928–1940*. Translated by Nicholas Walker. Cambridge: Polity, 1999.

4. Andrejevic, Mark. "The *Jouissance* of Trump." *Television and New Media* 17, no. 7 (2016): 651–655.

5. Benjamin, Walter. *The Arcades Project*. Edited and translated by Howard Eiland and Kevin McLaughlin. Cambridge, MA: Belknap/Harvard University Press, 1999.

6. — "The Author as Producer." In *Understanding Brecht*. Translated by Anna Bostock. London: Verso, 2003. 85–103.

7. — "Dream Kitsch: Gloss on Surrealism" (1925). In *The Work of Art in the Age of Its Technical Reproducibility and Other Writings*. Edited by Michael W. Jennings et al. Translated by Edmund Jephcott, Rodney Livingstone, Howard Eiland et al. Cambridge, MA: Belknap/Harvard University Press, 2008. 236–239.

8. — *Schriften*. Frankfurt am Main: Suhrkamp Verlag, 1955.

9. — "A Small History of Photography." In *One-Way Street and Other Writings*. Translated by Edmund Jephcott and Kingsley Shorter. London: Verso, 1999. 240–257.

10. — "The Storyteller." In *Illuminations*. Translated by Harry Zohn. London: Fontana, 1982. 83–109.

11. — "The Work of Art in the Age of Mechanical Reproduction," in *Illuminations,* ed. Hannah Arendt. London: Pimlico, 1999.

12. — "Surrealism" (1929). In *One-Way Street and Other Writings*. Translated by J. A. Underwood and edited by Amit Chaudhuri. London: Penguin, 2009. 143–160.

13. — "Theses on the Philosophy of History." In *Illuminations*. Translated by Harry Zohn. London: Fontana, 1982. 255–266.

14. *Understanding Brecht.* Translated by Anna Bostock. London: Verso, 1998.

15. — "The Work of Art in the Age of Mechanical Reproduction." In *One-Way Street and Other Writings.* Edited by Amit Chaudhuri and translated by J. A. Underwood. London and New York: Penguin, 2008. 228–259.

16. — "The Work of Art in the Age of Its Technological Reproducibility." In *The Work of Art in the Age of Its Technological Reproducibility and Other Writings on Media.* Edited by Michael W. Jennings, Brigid Doherty, Thomas Y. Levin. Cambridge, MA: Belknap/Harvard University Press, 2008. 19–55.

17. Berger, John. *Ways of Seeing.* London: Penguin, 1977.

18. Berkowitz, Roger, and Taun N. Toay, eds. *The Intellectual Origins of the Global Financial Crisis.* New York: Fordham University Press, 2013.

19. Binnet, Alexander. "Donald Trump and the Aesthetics of Fascism: What a 20th-century Marxist art critic can teach us about a very 21st-century candidate." *In These Times* (January 28, 2016). Accessed June 28, 2017. http://inthesetimes.com/article/18807/donald-trump-and-the-aesthetics-of-fascism.

20. Brownstein, Ronald. "Trump's rhetoric of white nostalgia." *The Atlantic* (June 2, 2016). Accessed June 30, 2017. https://www.theatlantic.com/politics/archive/2016/06/trumps-rhetoric-of-white-nostalgia/485192/.

21. Buck-Morss, Susan. "Revolutionary Time: The Vanguard and the Avant-Garde." In *Benjamin Studies, Studien 1.* Edited by Helga Geyer Ryan. Amsterdam: Rodopi, 2002.

22. Caughie, Pamela. *Virginia Woolf in the Age of Mechanical Reproduction.* London: Routledge, 2000.

23. Clarke, John. "Cultural Studies: a British inheritance." In *New Times and Old Enemies: Essays on Cultural Studies and America.* New York: Harper Collins, 1991.

24. Denby, David. "The Plot Against America: Trump's Rhetoric." *New Yorker* (Dec. 15, 2015). Accessed June 30, 2017. http://www.newyorker.com/culture/cultural-comment/plot-america-donald-trumps-rhetoric.

25. Dumm, Thomas. "Degraded fascism, nihilism, and Donald Trump." *Contemporary Condition* (September 2015). Accessed June 28, 2017. http:// contemporarycondition.

blogspot.co.uk/2015/09/degraded-fascism-nihilism-and-donald.html.

26. Duttlinger, Caroline. "Between Contemplation and Distraction: Configurations of Attention in Walter Benjamin." *German Studies Review* 30, no. 1 (February 2007): 33–54.

27. Eagleton, Terry. *Walter Benjamin; or, Towards a Revolutionary Criticism.* London: Verso, 1981.

28. Eiland, Howard, and Michael W. Jennings. *Walter Benjamin: A Critical Life.* Cambridge, MA: Belknap/Harvard University Press, 2013.

29. Feigel, Lara. *Literature, Cinema, and Politics 1930–1945: Reading Between the Frames.* Edinburgh University Press, 2010.

30. Foster, Peter. "The rise of the far-right in Europe is not a false alarm." *Telegraph* (May 19, 2016). Accessed June 30, 2017. http://www.telegraph.co.uk/news/2016/05/19/the-rise-of-the-far-right-in-europe-is-not-a-false-alarm/.

31. Franzen, Jonathan. *The Corrections.* London: Fourth Estate, 2001.

32. Goebel, Rolf. "Introduction: Benjamin's Actuality." In *A Companion to the Works of Walter Benjamin.* Edited by Rolf Goebel. London: Camden House, 2009. 1–22.

33. Goldstein, Donna M., and Kira Hall. "Postelection surrealism and nostalgic racism in the hands of Donald Trump." *HAU: Journal of Ethnographic Theory* 7, no. 1 (2017). http://dx.doi.org/10.14318/hau7.1.026.

34. Greenberg, Udi E. "The Politics of the Walter Benjamin Industry." *Theory, Culture & Society* 25, no. 3 (2008): 53–68. Accessed June 28, 2017. DOI: 10.1177/0263276408090657.

35. Gubster, Mike. *Time's Visible Surface: Alois Riegl and the Discourse on History and Temporality in Fin-de-Siécle Vienna.* Detroit, MI: Wayne State University Press, 2006.

36. Horkheimer, Max. "Traditional and Critical Theory" (1937). In *Selected Essays.* London and New York: Continuum, 1982. 188–244.

37. Jeffries, Stuart. "Why a forgotten 1930s critique of capitalism is back in fashion." *Guardian* (September 9, 2016). Accessed June 20, 2017. https:// www. theguardian.com/books/2016/sep/09/marxist-critique-capitalism-frankfurt-

school-cultural-apocalypse.

38. — *Grand Hotel Abyss: The Lives of the Frankfurt School.* London: Verso, 2016.

39. Jones, Oliver. *Donald Trump: The Rhetoric.* London: Eyeware Publishing, 2016.

40. Kang, Jaeho. *Walter Benjamin and the Media: The Spectacle of Modernity.* Cambridge: Polity Press, 2014.

41. Leith, Sam. "Trump's rhetoric: a triumph of inarticulacy." *Guardian* (January 13, 2017). Accessed June 30, 2017. https://www.theguardian.com/us-news/2017/jan/13/donald-trumps-rhetoric-how-being-inarticulate-is-seen-as-authentic.

42. Leslie, Esther. *Walter Benjamin: Overpowering Conformism.* London: Reaktion, 2000.

43. — *Walter Benjamin.* London: Reaktion, 2007.

44. "Revolutionary potential and Walter Benjamin: A postwar reception history." In *Critical Companion to Contemporary Marxism.* Edited by Gregory Elliot and Jacques Bidet. Leiden: Brill, 2007. 549–566.

45. — *Hollywood Flatlands, Critical Theory and the Avant-Garde.* London: Verso, 2002.

46. Levin, T. Y. "Walter Benjamin and the Theory of Art History." *October* 47 (Winter 1988): 77–83.

47. Lukács, Georg. *History and Class Consciousness: Studies in Marxist Dialectics.* London: Merlin, 1968 (1923). 83.

48. Mardell, Mark. "Fascism, the 1930s, and the 21st century." *BBC News* (December 20, 2016). Accessed June 30, 2017. http://www.bbc.co.uk/news/uk-politics-38317787.

49. Marinetti, Tommaso. "Futurist Manifesto" (1908). In *Theories of Modern Art: A Source Book by Artists and Critics.* Edited by Herschel B. Chipp. Berkeley, CA: University of California Press, 1996 (1968). 285–287 (286).

50. Marx, Karl. "The fetishism of commodities and the secret thereof." *Capital: Unabridged edition.* Edited by David McLellan. Oxford: Oxford University Press, 2008 (1867). 42–50.

51. McChesney, Robert W. "Whatever happened to cultural studies?" In *American*

Cultural Studies. Edited by Catherine A. Warren and Mary Douglas Vavrus. Chicago: University of Illinois Press, 2002. 76–93.

52. McDougall, James. "No, this isn't the 1930s—but yes, this is fascism." *The Conversation* (November 16, 2016). Accessed June 30, 2017. https://theconversation.com/no-this-isnt-the-1930s-but-yes-this-is-fascism-68867.

53. McRobbie, Angela. "The *Passagenwerk* and the place of Walter Benjamin in cultural studies. *Cultural Studies* 6, no. 2 (1992): 147–169. Reprinted in: *The Cultural Studies Reader.* Edited by Simon During. London: Routledge, 1999. 77–96.

54. Meissner, Miriam. *Narrating the Global Financial Crisis: Urban Imaginaries and the Politics of Myth.* New York and Basingstoke: Palgrave, 2017.

55. Mirowski, Philip. *Never Let a Serious Crisis Go to Waste: How Neoliberalism Survived the Financial Meltdown.* London: Verso, 2013.

56. Nelson, Cary. "Always Already Cultural Studies." In *English Studies/Cultural Studies: Institutionalizing Dissent.* Edited by Isaiah Smithson and Nancy Ruff. Chicago: University of Illinois Press, 1994. 191–206.

57. Ortile, Matt. "11 Wonderful Illuminating Quotes from Walter Benjamin: Get Ready for Some *Illuminations* in Honor of His 122nd Birthday Today!" *Buzzfeed* (July 15, 2014). Accessed June 30, 2017. https://www.buzzfeed.com/mattortile/work-of-art-in-the-age-of-social-discovery?utm_term=.vb8mqkAAj#.shK5pgyyD.

58. Palmer, John. "The rise of the far right parties across Europe is a chilling echo of the 1930s." *Guardian* (November 15, 2013). Accessed June 30, 2017. https://www.theguardian.com/commentisfree/2013/nov/15/far-right-threat-europe-integration.

59. Penney, Joel. *Citizen Marketer: Promoting Political Opinion in the Social Media Age* (Oxford: Oxford University Press, 2017), 113.

60. Pusca, Anca, ed. *Walter Benjamin and the Aesthetics of Change.* New York and Basingstoke: Palgrave Macmillan, 2010.

61. Robinson, Andrew. "Walter Benjamin and Critical Theory." *Ceasefire* (April 4, 2013). Accessed June 27, 2017. https://ceasefiremagazine.co.uk/in-theory-

benjamin-1/.

62. Roos, Jeremy. "Trump's victory speaks to a crumbling liberal order." *Roar* (November 9, 2016). Accessed June 20, 2017. https://roarmag.org/essays/ trump-victory-legitimation-crisis-capitalism/.

63. Ross, Alex. "The Frankfurt School Knew Trump Was Coming." *New Yorker* (December 5, 2016). Accessed June 20, 2017. http://www.newyorker.com/ culture/cultural-comment/the-frankfurt-school-knew-trump-was-coming.

64. Schiwy, Freya, and Alessandro Fornazzari, eds. *Digital Media, Cultural Production and Speculative Capitalism.* London: Routledge, 2013.

65. Shepherd, Laura J., and Caitlin Hamilton, eds. *Understanding Popular Culture and World Politics in the Digital Age.* London: Routledge, 2016.

66. Sontag, Susan. "The Decay of Cinema." *New York Times* (February 25, 1996). Accessed June 28, 2017. http://www.nytimes.com/books/00/03/12/specials/ sontag-cinema.html.

67. Valéry, Paul. "The Conquest of Ubiquity" (1928). In *Aesthetics.* Translated by Ralph Manheim. New York: Pantheon Books, 1964.

68. Vassiliou, Konstantinos. "The Aura of Art After the Advent of the Digital." In *Walter Benjamin and the Aesthetics of Change.* Edited by Anca Pusca. New York and Basingstoke: Palgrave Macmillan, 2010. 158–170.

69. Whyman, Tom. "Which Philosophy Can Best Explain 2016?" *Vice* (December 15, 2016). Accessed June 20, 2017. https://www.vice.com/en_uk/article/z4ngy4/ which-philosophy-can-help-us-understand-2016.

70. Wizislda, Erdmut. *Walter Benjamin and Bertolt Brecht: The Story of a Friendship.* Translated by Christine Shuttleworth. New Haven: Yale University Press, 2009.

71. Wolff, Janet. "Memoirs and Micrologies: Walter Benjamin, feminism, and cultural analysis." In *Walter Benjamin: Critical Interventions in Cultural Theory. Vol III: Appropriations.* Edited by Peter Osborne. London: Routledge, 2005. 319–333.

原书作者简介

瓦尔特·本雅明（1892-1940）是德国犹太裔左翼文化批评家和散文家，代表作有《机械复制时代的艺术作品》《历史哲学论纲》和未完成的作品《拱廊街计划》。本雅明是"法兰克福学派"成员——该学派由法兰克福大学社会研究所的一众学者组成。与本雅明一样，这些学者以文化生产、资本主义与社会之间的关系为研究焦点，并积极投身反法西斯运动。本雅明的论著主要探讨摄影和电影兴起以来，艺术变革所产生的政治影响及其接受面貌，因而难以划归任何一门学科，艺术史、文学、传媒和历史等不同领域的研究者都会征引其观点。本雅明在有生之年并未得到学界认可。他在逃避盖世太保追捕的途中自杀，但死因成谜。此后数十年间，他几乎被彻底埋没。如今，本雅明已是举世公认的批评理论家和文化研究学者，遥遥领先于他的时代。

本书作者简介

蕾切尔·迪妮是英国罗汉普顿大学英语文学专业讲师。她的研究领域包括先锋派文学、马克思主义文学批评和废弃物研究。她的首部专著《20世纪小说中的消费主义、废弃物和循环利用：先锋派的遗产》于2016年由帕尔格雷夫·麦克米伦出版公司出版。她先后获得剑桥大学学士学位、伦敦国王学院硕士学位和伦敦大学学院博士学位。

世界名著中的批判性思维

《世界思想宝库钥匙丛书》致力于深入浅出地阐释全世界著名思想家的观点，不论是谁、在何处都能了解到，从而推进批判性思维发展。

《世界思想宝库钥匙丛书》与世界顶尖大学的一流学者合作，为一系列学科中最有影响的著作推出新的分析文本，介绍其观点和影响。在这一不断扩展的系列中，每种选入的著作都代表了历经时间考验的思想典范。通过为这些著作提供必要背景、揭示原作者的学术渊源以及说明这些著作所产生的影响，本系列图书希望让读者以新视角看待这些划时代的经典之作。读者应学会思考、运用并挑战这些著作中的观点，而不是简单接受它们。

ABOUT THE AUTHOR OF THE ORIGINAL WORK

Walter Benjamin (1892–1940) was a leftist German Jewish cultural critic and essayist best known for "The Work of Art in the Age of Mechanical Reproduction," "Theses on the Philosophy of History," and his unfinished book, *The Arcades Project*. Benjamin is associated with the "Frankfurt School"—a group of scholars based at the Institute for Social Research at the University of Frankfurt. Like Benjamin, these scholars were concerned with the relationship between cultural production, capitalism, and society, and were actively engaged in opposing the rise of fascism. Difficult to categorize within any one discipline, and used by scholars in areas as various as art history, literary studies, media studies, and history, Benjamin's work probes the political ramifications of the transformation of art and its reception following the advent of photography and film. Unrecognized during his lifetime, and largely forgotten in the decades following his suspected suicide while fleeing the Gestapo, Benjamin is now recognized as a critical theorist and cultural studies scholar who was ahead of his time.

ABOUT THE AUTHOR OF THE ANALYSIS

Rachele Dini is a lecturer in English literature at the University of Roehampton. Her areas of specialty include literary avant-gardes, Marxist literary criticism, and discard studies. Her first book, *Consumerism, Waste and Re-use in Twentieth-Century Fiction: Legacies of the Avant-Garde*, was published by Palgrave Macmillan in 2016. She received her undergraduate degree from the University of Cambridge, her MA from King's College, London, and her PhD from UCL.

ABOUT MACAT
GREAT WORKS FOR CRITICAL THINKING

Macat is focused on making the ideas of the world's great thinkers accessible and comprehensible to everybody, everywhere, in ways that promote the development of enhanced critical thinking skills.

It works with leading academics from the world's top universities to produce new analyses that focus on the ideas and the impact of the most influential works ever written across a wide variety of academic disciplines. Each of the works that sit at the heart of its growing library is an enduring example of great thinking. But by setting them in context — and looking at the influences that shaped their authors, as well as the responses they provoked — Macat encourages readers to look at these classics and game-changers with fresh eyes. Readers learn to think, engage and challenge their ideas, rather than simply accepting them.

批判性思维与《机械复制时代的艺术作品》

首要批判性思维技巧：创造性思维

次要批判性思维技巧：理性化思维

瓦尔特·本雅明是创造性思想家的典型代表。在《机械复制时代的艺术作品》中，他列举了一系列看似毫不相干的现象——电影和摄影发明孕育的诸多可能性，法西斯主义对"景观"的依赖，艺术文学对新兴技术的期待——并以崭新的视角将它们串联在一起，提出艺术批评的全新理论。本雅明这篇作品的十四个命题，以及后记中作出的惊人结论，并非以线性逻辑一以贯之，而且该文本身更是难以归类。这是一篇艺术评论，却迥异于同时代批评家们的论作。本雅明直截了当地指出，那些人已经彻底落伍。相反，《机械复制时代的艺术作品》旨在批判资本主义制度下法西斯主义对新兴媒介的滥用。针对马克思主义学者对大众文化的批判，本雅明持有异议。实际上，在他看来，观看电影恰恰能使大众在面对意识形态宣传时，更具怀疑精神和批判意识。只可惜，他的思想蕴藉在诗意的语言和意象、华丽的词藻，以及令人惊叹的类比之中，这会让某些哲学家感到困惑。

《机械复制时代的艺术作品》堪称本雅明"星丛思想"的典范——他曾用这个术语描述自己的思考方式，即提出一系列观点，而不是一个最终论断。本雅明渴望有朝一日能写出一本完全由引文片段组成的著作，这正是其思维模式的体现。这种模式其实是在模仿他最崇拜的那些艺术家，他们采用片断式、实验性的方法来思考问题——然而，从他那个时代，乃至当今的学术写作来看，这一切都显得格格不入。

CRITICAL THINKING AND "THE WORK OF ART IN THE AGE OF MECHANICAL REPRODUCTION"

- Primary critical thinking skill: CREATIVE THINKING
- Secondary critical thinking skill: REASONING

Walter Benjamin is a prime example of a creative thinker. In "The Work of Art in the Age of Mechanical Reproduction," he sets out a series of seemingly unrelated phenomena—the possibilities opened up by the advent of film and photography, fascism's reliance on spectacle, and art and literature's anticipation of new technologies—and connects them in new ways to propose a novel theory of art criticism. The fourteen strands of Benjamin's thesis, and the surprising conclusions he draws in his epilogue, do not progress in a linear way and the essay itself is impossible to classify. This is art criticism, but not like that proposed by his contemporaries, whom he explicitly says are outdated. Rather, "The Work of Art in the Age of Mechanical Reproduction" is a critique of fascism's adoption of the new media developed under capitalism. Benjamin takes issue with his fellow Marxists' critiques of mass culture, since he actually thinks that by watching movies, people can learn to be *more* skeptical and critical of propaganda. His thinking, alas, relies on poetic language and imagery, florid turns of phrase, and startling analogies that would leave some philosophers puzzled.

"The Work of Art" is an example of Benjamin's "constellatory thinking"—a term he used to describe his tendency to produce a cluster of ideas rather than one final statement. The fact that Benjamin aspired to one day write a book entirely composed of fragments of quotations reflects this same approach. This thinking imitates the fragmentary, experimental approach of the artists he most admired—but it is a far cry from the academic writing of his contemporaries or, indeed, of today.

《世界思想宝库钥匙丛书》简介

《世界思想宝库钥匙丛书》致力于为一系列在各领域产生重大影响的人文社科类经典著作提供独特的学术探讨。每一本读物都不仅仅是原经典著作的内容摘要，而是介绍并深入研究原经典著作的学术渊源、主要观点和历史影响。这一丛书的目的是提供一套学习资料，以促进读者掌握批判性思维，从而更全面、深刻地去理解重要思想。

每一本读物分为3个部分：学术渊源、学术思想和学术影响，每个部分下有4个小节。这些章节旨在从各个方面研究原经典著作及其反响。

由于独特的体例，每一本读物不但易于阅读，而且另有一项优点：所有读物的编排体例相同，读者在进行某个知识层面的调查或研究时可交叉参阅多本该丛书中的相关读物，从而开启跨领域研究的路径。

为了方便阅读，每本读物最后还列出了术语表和人名表（在书中则以星号＊标记），此外还有参考文献。

《世界思想宝库钥匙丛书》与剑桥大学合作，理清了批判性思维的要点，即如何通过6种技能来进行有效思考。其中3种技能让我们能够理解问题，另3种技能让我们有能力解决问题。这6种技能合称为"批判性思维PACIER模式"，它们是：

分析：了解如何建立一个观点；
评估：研究一个观点的优点和缺点；
阐释：对意义所产生的问题加以理解；
创造性思维：提出新的见解，发现新的联系；
解决问题：提出切实有效的解决办法；
理性化思维：创建有说服力的观点。

THE MACAT LIBRARY

The Macat Library is a series of unique academic explorations of seminal works in the humanities and social sciences — books and papers that have had a significant and widely recognised impact on their disciplines. It has been created to serve as much more than just a summary of what lies between the covers of a great book. It illuminates and explores the influences on, ideas of, and impact of that book. Our goal is to offer a learning resource that encourages critical thinking and fosters a better, deeper understanding of important ideas.

Each publication is divided into three Sections: Influences, Ideas, and Impact. Each Section has four Modules. These explore every important facet of the work, and the responses to it.

This Section-Module structure makes a Macat Library book easy to use, but it has another important feature. Because each Macat book is written to the same format, it is possible (and encouraged!) to cross-reference multiple Macat books along the same lines of inquiry or research. This allows the reader to open up interesting interdisciplinary pathways.

To further aid your reading, lists of glossary terms and people mentioned are included at the end of this book (these are indicated by an asterisk [*] throughout) — as well as a list of works cited.

Macat has worked with the University of Cambridge to identify the elements of critical thinking and understand the ways in which six different skills combine to enable effective thinking.

Three allow us to fully understand a problem; three more give us the tools to solve it. Together, these six skills make up the PACIER model of critical thinking. They are:

ANALYSIS — understanding how an argument is built
EVALUATION — exploring the strengths and weaknesses of an argument
INTERPRETATION — understanding issues of meaning
CREATIVE THINKING — coming up with new ideas and fresh connections
PROBLEM-SOLVING — producing strong solutions
REASONING — creating strong arguments

"《世界思想宝库钥匙丛书》提供了独一无二的跨学科学习和研究工具。它介绍那些革新了各自学科研究的经典著作，还邀请全世界一流专家和教育机构进行严谨的分析，为每位读者打开世界顶级教育的大门。"

—— 安德烈亚斯·施莱歇尔，
经济合作与发展组织教育与技能司司长

"《世界思想宝库钥匙丛书》直面大学教育的巨大挑战……他们组建了一支精干而活跃的学者队伍，来推出在研究广度上颇具新意的教学材料。"

—— 布罗尔斯教授、勋爵，剑桥大学前校长

"《世界思想宝库钥匙丛书》的愿景令人赞叹。它通过分析和阐释那些曾深刻影响人类思想以及社会、经济发展的经典文本，提供了新的学习方法。它推动批判性思维，这对于任何社会和经济体来说都是至关重要的。这就是未来的学习方法。"

—— 查尔斯·克拉克阁下，英国前教育大臣

"对于那些影响了各自领域的著作，《世界思想宝库钥匙丛书》能让人们立即了解到围绕那些著作展开的评论性言论，这让该系列图书成为在这些领域从事研究的师生们不可或缺的资源。"

—— 威廉·特朗佐教授，加利福尼亚大学圣地亚哥分校

"Macat offers an amazing first-of-its-kind tool for interdisciplinary learning and research. Its focus on works that transformed their disciplines and its rigorous approach, drawing on the world's leading experts and educational institutions, opens up a world-class education to anyone."

—— Andreas Schleicher, Director for Education and Skills, Organisation for Economic Co-operation and Development

"Macat is taking on some of the major challenges in university education... They have drawn together a strong team of active academics who are producing teaching materials that are novel in the breadth of their approach."

—— Prof Lord Broers, former Vice-Chancellor of the University of Cambridge

"The Macat vision is exceptionally exciting. It focuses upon new modes of learning which analyse and explain seminal texts which have profoundly influenced world thinking and so social and economic development. It promotes the kind of critical thinking which is essential for any society and economy. This is the learning of the future."

—— Rt Hon Charles Clarke, former UK Secretary of State for Education

"The Macat analyses provide immediate access to the critical conversation surrounding the books that have shaped their respective discipline, which will make them an invaluable resource to all of those, students and teachers, working in the field."

—— Professor William Tronzo, University of California at San Diego

♀ The Macat Library
世界思想宝库钥匙丛书

TITLE	中文书名	类别
An Analysis of Arjun Appadurai's *Modernity at Large: Cultural Dimensions of Globalization*	解析阿尔君·阿帕杜莱《消失的现代性：全球化的文化维度》	人类学
An Analysis of Claude Lévi-Strauss's *Structural Anthropology*	解析克劳德·列维-斯特劳斯《结构人类学》	人类学
An Analysis of Marcel Mauss's *The Gift*	解析马塞尔·莫斯《礼物》	人类学
An Analysis of Jared M. Diamond's *Guns, Germs, and Steel: The Fate of Human Societies*	解析贾雷德·戴蒙德《枪炮、病菌与钢铁：人类社会的命运》	人类学
An Analysis of Clifford Geertz's *The Interpretation of Cultures*	解析克利福德·格尔茨《文化的解释》	人类学
An Analysis of Philippe Ariès's *Centuries of Childhood: A Social History of Family Life*	解析菲力浦·阿利埃斯《儿童的世纪：旧制度下的儿童和家庭生活》	人类学
An Analysis of W. Chan Kim & Renée Mauborgne's *Blue Ocean Strategy*	解析金伟灿/勒妮·莫博涅《蓝海战略》	商业
An Analysis of John P. Kotter's *Leading Change*	解析约翰·P.科特《领导变革》	商业
An Analysis of Michael E. Porter's *Competitive Strategy: Techniques for Analyzing Industries and Competitors*	解析迈克尔·E.波特《竞争战略：分析产业和竞争对手的技术》	商业
An Analysis of Jean Lave & Etienne Wenger's *Situated Learning: Legitimate Peripheral Participation*	解析琼·莱夫/艾蒂纳·温格《情境学习：合法的边缘性参与》	商业
An Analysis of Douglas McGregor's *The Human Side of Enterprise*	解析道格拉斯·麦格雷戈《企业的人性面》	商业
An Analysis of Milton Friedman's *Capitalism and Freedom*	解析米尔顿·弗里德曼《资本主义与自由》	商业
An Analysis of Ludwig von Mises's *The Theory of Money and Credit*	解析路德维希·冯·米塞斯《货币和信用理论》	经济学
An Analysis of Adam Smith's *The Wealth of Nations*	解析亚当·斯密《国富论》	经济学
An Analysis of Thomas Piketty's *Capital in the Twenty-First Century*	解析托马斯·皮凯蒂《21世纪资本论》	经济学
An Analysis of Nassim Nicholas Taleb's *The Black Swan: The Impact of the Highly Improbable*	解析纳西姆·尼古拉斯·塔勒布《黑天鹅：如何应对不可预知的未来》	经济学
An Analysis of Ha-Joon Chang's *Kicking Away the Ladder*	解析张夏准《富国陷阱：发达国家为何踢开梯子》	经济学
An Analysis of Thomas Robert Malthus's *An Essay on the Principle of Population*	解析托马斯·罗伯特·马尔萨斯《人口论》	经济学

An Analysis of John Maynard Keynes's *The General Theory of Employment, Interest and Money*	解析约翰·梅纳德·凯恩斯《就业、利息和货币通论》	经济学
An Analysis of Milton Friedman's *The Role of Monetary Policy*	解析米尔顿·弗里德曼《货币政策的作用》	经济学
An Analysis of Burton G. Malkiel's *A Random Walk Down Wall Street*	解析伯顿·G. 马尔基尔《漫步华尔街》	经济学
An Analysis of Friedrich A. Hayek's *The Road to Serfdom*	解析弗里德里希·A. 哈耶克《通往奴役之路》	经济学
An Analysis of Charles P. Kindleberger's *Manias, Panics, and Crashes: A History of Financial Crises*	解析查尔斯·P. 金德尔伯格《疯狂、惊恐和崩溃：金融危机史》	经济学
An Analysis of Amartya Sen's *Development as Freedom*	解析阿马蒂亚·森《以自由看待发展》	经济学
An Analysis of Rachel Carson's *Silent Spring*	解析蕾切尔·卡森《寂静的春天》	地理学
An Analysis of Charles Darwin's *On the Origin of Species: by Means of Natural Selection, or The Preservation of Favoured Races in the Struggle for Life*	解析查尔斯·达尔文《物种起源》	地理学
An Analysis of World Commission on Environment and Development's *The Brundtland Report, Our Common Future*	解析世界环境与发展委员会《布伦特兰报告：我们共同的未来》	地理学
An Analysis of James E. Lovelock's *Gaia: A New Look at Life on Earth*	解析詹姆斯·E. 拉伍洛克《盖娅：地球生命的新视野》	地理学
An Analysis of Paul Kennedy's *The Rise and Fall of the Great Powers: Economic Change and Military Conflict from 1500—2000*	解析保罗·肯尼迪《大国的兴衰：1500—2000 年的经济变革与军事冲突》	历史
An Analysis of Janet L. Abu-Lughod's *Before European Hegemony: The World System A. D. 1250—1350*	解析珍妮特·L. 阿布-卢格霍德《欧洲霸权之前：1250—1350 年的世界体系》	历史
An Analysis of Alfred W. Crosby's *The Columbian Exchange: Biological and Cultural Consequences of 1492*	解析艾尔弗雷德·W. 克罗斯比《哥伦布大交换：1492 年以后的生物影响和文化冲击》	历史
An Analysis of Tony Judt's *Postwar: A History of Europe since 1945*	解析托尼·朱特《战后欧洲史》	历史
An Analysis of Richard J. Evans's *In Defence of History*	解析理查德·J. 艾文斯《捍卫历史》	历史
An Analysis of Eric Hobsbawm's *The Age of Revolution: Europe 1789–1848*	解析艾瑞克·霍布斯鲍姆《革命的年代：欧洲 1789—1848 年》	历史

An Analysis of Roland Barthes's *Mythologies*	解析罗兰·巴特《神话学》	文学与批判理论
An Analysis of Simone de Beauvoir's *The Second Sex*	解析西蒙娜·德·波伏娃《第二性》	文学与批判理论
An Analysis of Edward W. Said's *Orientalism*	解析爱德华·W. 萨义德《东方主义》	文学与批判理论
An Analysis of Virginia Woolf's *A Room of One's Own*	解析弗吉尼亚·伍尔芙《一间自己的房间》	文学与批判理论
An Analysis of Judith Butler's *Gender Trouble*	解析朱迪斯·巴特勒《性别麻烦》	文学与批判理论
An Analysis of Ferdinand de Saussure's *Course in General Linguistics*	解析费尔迪南·德·索绪尔《普通语言学教程》	文学与批判理论
An Analysis of Susan Sontag's *On Photography*	解析苏珊·桑塔格《论摄影》	文学与批判理论
An Analysis of Walter Benjamin's *The Work of Art in the Age of Mechanical Reproduction*	解析瓦尔特·本雅明《机械复制时代的艺术作品》	文学与批判理论
An Analysis of W.E.B. Du Bois's *The Souls of Black Folk*	解析 W.E.B. 杜波依斯《黑人的灵魂》	文学与批判理论
An Analysis of Plato's *The Republic*	解析柏拉图《理想国》	哲学
An Analysis of Plato's *Symposium*	解析柏拉图《会饮篇》	哲学
An Analysis of Aristotle's *Metaphysics*	解析亚里士多德《形而上学》	哲学
An Analysis of Aristotle's *Nicomachean Ethics*	解析亚里士多德《尼各马可伦理学》	哲学
An Analysis of Immanuel Kant's *Critique of Pure Reason*	解析伊曼努尔·康德《纯粹理性批判》	哲学
An Analysis of Ludwig Wittgenstein's *Philosophical Investigations*	解析路德维希·维特根斯坦《哲学研究》	哲学
An Analysis of G.W.F. Hegel's *Phenomenology of Spirit*	解析 G.W.F. 黑格尔《精神现象学》	哲学
An Analysis of Baruch Spinoza's *Ethics*	解析巴鲁赫·斯宾诺莎《伦理学》	哲学
An Analysis of Hannah Arendt's *The Human Condition*	解析汉娜·阿伦特《人的境况》	哲学
An Analysis of G.E.M. Anscombe's *Modern Moral Philosophy*	解析 G.E.M. 安斯康姆《现代道德哲学》	哲学
An Analysis of David Hume's *An Enquiry Concerning Human Understanding*	解析大卫·休谟《人类理解研究》	哲学

An Analysis of Søren Kierkegaard's *Fear and Trembling*	解析索伦·克尔凯郭尔《恐惧与战栗》	哲学
An Analysis of René Descartes's *Meditations on First Philosophy*	解析勒内·笛卡尔《第一哲学沉思录》	哲学
An Analysis of Friedrich Nietzsche's *On the Genealogy of Morality*	解析弗里德里希·尼采《论道德的谱系》	哲学
An Analysis of Gilbert Ryle's *The Concept of Mind*	解析吉尔伯特·赖尔《心的概念》	哲学
An Analysis of Thomas Kuhn's *The Structure of Scientific Revolutions*	解析托马斯·库恩《科学革命的结构》	哲学
An Analysis of John Stuart Mill's *Utilitarianism*	解析约翰·斯图亚特·穆勒《功利主义》	哲学
An Analysis of Aristotle's *Politics*	解析亚里士多德《政治学》	政治学
An Analysis of Niccolò Machiavelli's *The Prince*	解析尼科洛·马基雅维利《君主论》	政治学
An Analysis of Karl Marx's *Capital*	解析卡尔·马克思《资本论》	政治学
An Analysis of Benedict Anderson's *Imagined Communities*	解析本尼迪克特·安德森《想象的共同体》	政治学
An Analysis of Samuel P. Huntington's *The Clash of Civilizations and the Remaking of World Order*	解析塞缪尔·P.亨廷顿《文明的冲突与世界秩序的重建》	政治学
An Analysis of Alexis de Tocqueville's *Democracy in America*	解析阿列克西·德·托克维尔《论美国的民主》	政治学
An Analysis of John A. Hobson's *Imperialism: A Study*	解析约翰·A.霍布森《帝国主义》	政治学
An Analysis of Thomas Paine's *Common Sense*	解析托马斯·潘恩《常识》	政治学
An Analysis of John Rawls's *A Theory of Justice*	解析约翰·罗尔斯《正义论》	政治学
An Analysis of Francis Fukuyama's *The End of History and the Last Man*	解析弗朗西斯·福山《历史的终结与最后的人》	政治学
An Analysis of John Locke's *Two Treatises of Government*	解析约翰·洛克《政府论》	政治学
An Analysis of Sun Tzu's *The Art of War*	解析孙武《孙子兵法》	政治学
An Analysis of Henry Kissinger's *World Order: Reflections on the Character of Nations and the Course of History*	解析亨利·基辛格《世界秩序》	政治学
An Analysis of Jean-Jacques Rousseau's *The Social Contract*	解析让-雅克·卢梭《社会契约论》	政治学

An Analysis of Odd Arne Westad's *The Global Cold War: Third World Interventions and the Making of Our Times*	解析文安立《全球冷战：美苏对第三世界的干涉与当代世界的形成》	政治学
An Analysis of Sigmund Freud's *The Interpretation of Dreams*	解析西格蒙德·弗洛伊德《梦的解析》	心理学
An Analysis of William James' *The Principles of Psychology*	解析威廉·詹姆斯《心理学原理》	心理学
An Analysis of Philip Zimbardo's *The Lucifer Effect*	解析菲利普·津巴多《路西法效应》	心理学
An Analysis of Leon Festinger's *A Theory of Cognitive Dissonance*	解析利昂·费斯汀格《认知失调论》	心理学
An Analysis of Richard H. Thaler & Cass R. Sunstein's *Nudge: Improving Decisions about Health, Wealth, and Happiness*	解析理查德·H.泰勒/卡斯·R.桑斯坦《助推：如何做出有关健康、财富和幸福的更优决策》	心理学
An Analysis of Gordon Allport's *The Nature of Prejudice*	解析高尔登·奥尔波特《偏见的本质》	心理学
An Analysis of Steven Pinker's *The Better Angels of Our Nature: Why Violence Has Declined*	解析斯蒂芬·平克《人性中的善良天使：暴力为什么会减少》	心理学
An Analysis of Stanley Milgram's *Obedience to Authority*	解析斯坦利·米尔格拉姆《对权威的服从》	心理学
An Analysis of Betty Friedan's *The Feminine Mystique*	解析贝蒂·弗里丹《女性的奥秘》	心理学
An Analysis of David Riesman's *The Lonely Crowd: A Study of the Changing American Character*	解析大卫·理斯曼《孤独的人群：美国人社会性格演变之研究》	社会学
An Analysis of Franz Boas's *Race, Language and Culture*	解析弗朗兹·博厄斯《种族、语言与文化》	社会学
An Analysis of Pierre Bourdieu's *Outline of a Theory of Practice*	解析皮埃尔·布尔迪厄《实践理论大纲》	社会学
An Analysis of Max Weber's *The Protestant Ethic and the Spirit of Capitalism*	解析马克斯·韦伯《新教伦理与资本主义精神》	社会学
An Analysis of Jane Jacobs's *The Death and Life of Great American Cities*	解析简·雅各布斯《美国大城市的死与生》	社会学
An Analysis of C. Wright Mills's *The Sociological Imagination*	解析C.赖特·米尔斯《社会学的想象力》	社会学
An Analysis of Robert E. Lucas Jr.'s *Why Doesn't Capital Flow from Rich to Poor Countries?*	解析小罗伯特·E.卢卡斯《为何资本不从富国流向穷国？》	社会学

An Analysis of Émile Durkheim's *On Suicide*	解析埃米尔·迪尔凯姆《自杀论》	社会学
An Analysis of Eric Hoffer's *The True Believer: Thoughts on the Nature of Mass Movements*	解析埃里克·霍弗《狂热分子：群众运动圣经》	社会学
An Analysis of Jared M. Diamond's *Collapse: How Societies Choose to Fail or Survive*	解析贾雷德·M.戴蒙德《大崩溃：社会如何选择兴亡》	社会学
An Analysis of Michel Foucault's *The History of Sexuality Vol. 1: The Will to Knowledge*	解析米歇尔·福柯《性史（第一卷）：求知意志》	社会学
An Analysis of Michel Foucault's *Discipline and Punish*	解析米歇尔·福柯《规训与惩罚》	社会学
An Analysis of Richard Dawkins's *The Selfish Gene*	解析理查德·道金斯《自私的基因》	社会学
An Analysis of Antonio Gramsci's *Prison Notebooks*	解析安东尼奥·葛兰西《狱中札记》	社会学
An Analysis of Augustine's *Confessions*	解析奥古斯丁《忏悔录》	神学
An Analysis of C. S. Lewis's *The Abolition of Man*	解析 C. S. 路易斯《人之废》	神学

图书在版编目（CIP）数据

解析瓦尔特·本雅明《机械复制时代的艺术作品》：
汉、英 / 蕾切尔·迪妮 (Rachele Dini) 著；顾忆青译. --
上海：上海外语教育出版社，2020 (2023重印)
（世界思想宝库钥匙丛书）
ISBN 978-7-5446-6124-9

Ⅰ.①解… Ⅱ.①蕾… ②顾… Ⅲ.①本雅明
(Benjamin, Walter 1892-1940)—艺术理论—研究—汉、英
Ⅳ.①B516.59 ②J0

中国版本图书馆CIP数据核字（2020）第014561号

出版发行：**上海外语教育出版社**
（上海外国语大学内）　邮编：200083
电　　话：021-65425300（总机）
电子邮箱：bookinfo@sflep.com.cn
网　　址：http://www.sflep.com
责任编辑：石东利

印　　刷：上海信老印刷厂
开　　本：890×1240　1/32　印张 6.75　字数 138千字
版　　次：2020 年 6月第 1版　　2023 年 7月第 2次印刷

书　　号：ISBN 978-7-5446-6124-9
定　　价：30.00 元

本版图书如有印装质量问题，可向本社调换
质量服务热线：4008-213-263